The Nature of God

The Nature of God

David Yonggi Cho

Charisma®
HOUSE
Books about Spirit-Led Living

THE NATURE OF GOD by David Yonggi Cho
Published by Charisma House
A part of Strang Communications Company
600 Rinehart Road
Lake Mary, Florida 32746
www.charismahouse.com

Unless otherwise noted, all Scripture quotations are from the
Holy Bible, New International Version. Copyright © 1973, 1978,
1984, International Bible Society. Used by permission.

Scripture portions marked KJV are from the King James
Version of the Bible.

Cover design by Pat Theriault

Library of Congress Catalog Card Number: 2001090824
International Standard Book Number: 0-88419-773-5

01 02 03 04   8 7 6 5 4 3 2 1
Printed in the United States of America

Contents

Foreword by Dr. Max F. Morris . . . .*vii*

Part One: God the Father

1 The Character of the Father 1

2 The Ways of the Father 13

3 The Authority of the Father 27

4 The Compassion of the Father 37

5 The Blessings of the Father 53

Part Two: God the Son

6 The Gift of the Son 67

7 The Authority of the Son 81

8 The Ministry of the Son 91

9 The Sacrifice of the Son 99

10 The Victory of the Son 113

11 The Legacy of the Son 127

Part Three: God the Holy Spirit

12 The Personality of the Holy Spirit 139

13 The Work of the Holy Spirit 151

14 The Baptism of the Holy Spirit 167

15 The Evidence of the Holy Spirit 183

16 The Life of the Holy Spirit 195

FOREWORD

There are four unique doctrines of biblical theology that separate Christianity from all other world religions:

- The Incarnation (God the Son became human flesh)

- The Crucifixion (God the Son died for mankind's sin)

- The Resurrection (God the Son rose victoriously over death)

- The Trinity (one God in three persons: Father, Son and Holy Spirit)

Of these four, the doctrine of the Trinity—God the Father, God the Son and God the Holy Spirit—is the most distinctive and incomprehensible of them all. How can one God be three Persons? Through centuries of church history, Bible scholars and theologians have attempted to answer the question, but all attempts have fallen short. Utilizing the usual tools of empiricism there is no logical explanation. The bottom line is this—accepting the doctrine of the Trinity is not a matter of logic and explanation; it is a matter of faith.

Dr. David Yonggi Cho, a successful Korean pastor of a church with more than seven hundred thousand members, does not try to explain the Trinity. In this book, *The Nature of God*, he accepts the Trinity as a faith judgment. Why should one be required to explain empirically something that he has experienced? Dr. Cho has met and experienced the Father, Son and Holy Spirit. The three Persons are active in his life and affect his dynamic ministry.

Dr. Cho brings the Trinity alive, showing how the three persons of the Trinity affect the lives of believers. Or, to put it another way, he does not waste our time with novel abstractions or empty speculations. Rather, using a generous portion of the Word of God, he gives us a practical application of the Trinity in the life of every believer.

You cannot read this book and walk away indifferently. The book is captivating, making a lasting impact and revealing to the reader the reality of the Trinity—Father, Son and Holy Spirit. Any individual, whether pastor, evangelist, Bible teacher, ordinary Christian or nonbeliever, will be greatly blessed by reading *The Nature of God*. By faithfully applying the principles of this book, you will experience an enormous growth in your ministry.

–Dr. Max F. Morris

Part One
God the Father

ONE

The Character of the Father

Man's greatest tragedy is that his relationship with God has been shattered. As a result, he is no longer able to communicate with God. Originally, man knew God intimately; he had been created for the purpose of communicating and living in joy with God. But because of sin, his relationship with the Father was severed.

The Old Testament prophet Hosea shouted to the unrepentant Israelites, "Let us acknowledge the LORD; let us press on to acknowledge him. As surely as the sun rises, he will appear; he will come to us like the winter rains, like the spring rains that water the earth" (Hos. 6:3). In order to acknowledge the Lord, however, we must first know who He is and how He works.

It is not possible to know God through any of our senses. God cannot be seen, heard or felt. Therefore, we must learn of Him through His Word–the Bible.

WHO IS GOD?

Some people believe that Jehovah is a judgmental God. But it was God the Father who sent us Jesus Christ because of His love. It was God who redeemed our souls from judgment through the blood of Jesus Christ. It is God who protects us through the presence of the Holy Spirit. If we do not know and understand God correctly, we cannot commune in depth with Him, nor can we expect to receive His blessings.

THE GOD OF ABRAHAM

The God of Abraham is the "God who cares." God called Abraham out from the land of idols. Not only did He choose Abraham, but He also revealed to Abraham His will and purpose. He led Abraham throughout his life.

God allowed Abraham to establish his roots in Canaan and allowed his descendants to flourish in Canaan. And through the genealogy of one of Abraham's descendants, King David, the Messiah was born. How does the God of Abraham affect us, and what does He mean to us today?

The God of the Abraham is a caring God. He has planned and chosen His children from the beginning. Just as He cared for Abraham all the years of his life, He also cares for us and has predestined all of our lives. The psalmist wrote, "Such knowledge is too wonderful for me, too lofty for me to attain" (Ps. 139:6).

Although we may not realize it, God has already planned each of our lives. We must in return be led by God's tremendous care so that as we live our lives, we glorify God.

THE GOD OF ISAAC

The God of Isaac is the "God who provides." God said to childless Abraham, "Your wife Sarah will bear you a son, and you will call him Isaac. I will establish my covenant with him as an everlasting covenant for his descendants after him" (Gen. 17:19).

Through God's work, Abraham begot his son Isaac at the age of one hundred. But after Isaac had become an adolescent, God commanded Abraham to offer Isaac as a sacrifice. Upon hearing God's command, Abraham obeyed. He went up to the mountain God had chosen, built an altar and bound Isaac upon the altar. He then raised his knife to plunge into Isaac. Then Abraham heard God's voice: "Do not lay a hand on the boy . . . Do not do anything to him. Now I know that you fear God, because you have not withheld from me your son, your only son" (Gen. 22:12).

Abraham looked around and saw a ram whose horns were tangled in the bushes. Abraham offered the ram as a sacrifice. Abraham then named the place *Jehovah-jireh*, "the Lord Will Provide." He obeyed God to the fullest and received overflowing blessings from God as a gift. Later, Isaac, at the age of forty, married Rebekah and continued the unfinished work of Abraham.

The God of Isaac is the same God we know today. If we fully believe and obey God, we shall receive uncountable blessings like Isaac.

THE GOD OF JACOB

Jacob's God is "God who destroys." Jacob at one time relied on his wit, which resulted in his having to suffer unspeakable agony. However, following such ordeals, he became God's humble servant. With a bowl of porridge, Jacob wrested his brother Esau's right to his inheritance, and he deceived his father. Being fearful of his brother's wrath, Jacob escaped to his maternal uncle for protection. There, he himself was deceived by his uncle to spend the next twenty years in bone-grinding toil, after which he was finally able to return home with his family and a herd of animals (Gen. 31:40–55).

Still fearful of his brother's wrath, Jacob wrestled all night with God's angel, a struggle of life and death. During the struggle, the angel hit Jacob's hipbone and caused him to become a cripple for the rest of his life. In fact, it was after this struggle that Jacob was given the name of "Israel" and obtained a faith that caused him to be wholly dependent on God (Gen. 32:28). Thus, Jacob's life was one of continual

3

shattering. Through such hardships, Jacob's ego was shattered, but he was strengthened with a faith that depended wholly on God. He eventually became the father of the twelve tribes of Israel (Gen. 35:9–12).

Even today, God shatters our ego and selfishness through hardship and suffering. This molds us closer into the image of Christ, and we are ready to be used as God's servant to carry out His plans. The Father has a caring nature for all things, and He offers blessings for those who believe and obey. Through hardships, He molds us in the shape of Jesus Christ.

OUR GOOD FATHER

Because of God's molding us in the shape or image of Christ, many Christians cannot believe that "God is good." Some associate Him with fear and punishment. They think that He likes to make us suffer, that the Father resides somewhere far away and has no concern for us. This prevents people from having a deep and personal relationship with Him.

The apostle Paul wrote to the Ephesians, "Now to him who is able to do immeasurably more than all we ask or imagine, according to his power that is at work within us" (Eph. 3:20). In order to have a deep and personal relationship with God the Father, we must first overhaul our mistaken beliefs.

First, we must learn through the Bible that the Father is a good God. If we have read the Bible from Genesis to Revelation correctly, none of us would deny the fact that our Father God is good.

Also, we learn about our God through Jesus Christ. Jesus said, "Don't you know me, Philip, even after I have been among you such a long time? Anyone who has seen me has seen the Father" (John 14:9). Every place where Jesus went, He forgave sinners, drove out evil spirits, healed the sick and raised the dead. And following the will of the Father, Jesus sacrificed His life on the cross to give salvation to all people. When we look at the immense goodness of Jesus Christ, we can be certain that the Father's goodness is without limits.

Jesus also said, "Which of you, if his son asks for bread, will give him a stone? Or if he asks for a fish, will give him a snake? If you, then, though you are evil, know how to give good gifts to your children, how much more will your Father in heaven give good gifts to those who ask Him!" (Matt. 7:9–11). Jesus described God as a Father who gives good gifts. Knowing this, we must correct the misunderstanding that we have of God. Then, we can have a deep and personal relationship with Him.

The Father also does good through cooperation. The Bible says, "And we know that in all things God works for the good of those who love him, who have been called according to his purpose" (Rom. 8:28). Those who have been called by God and follow His will are those who truly love God.

How can we know whether we ourselves love God? First John 5:3 says, "This is love for God: to obey his commands. And his commands are not burdensome." If we love God, we must live according to the Bible. Jesus told us to put love into practice. We must live with love for God and our neighbors by helping the needy and spreading the gospel. When we love God, He fulfills His goodness and mercy through our cooperation.

THE RIGHTEOUS GOD

Just because "God is good" does not mean that He will close His eyes and accept us blindly when we live according to our own will and commit sin. Because He is a righteous God, when we commit sins, we cannot escape His judgment.

At the cross we witness clearly the righteousness of God. God willed His only begotten Son, Jesus Christ, to bear the cross. He willed Jesus to bear the sins of man. And He judged Jesus Christ mercilessly. The agony on the cross caused Jesus to cry, "My God, my God, why have you forsaken me?" (Matt. 27:46).

Why did Jesus Christ have to bear such anguish? It was to redeem us and pay for our sins through death. In order for us to have a personal relationship with God, we must turn away from sinful ways. He does not negotiate or compromise. No matter how insignificant the sin, He does not look the other way. First Thessalonians 5:22 says, "Avoid every kind of evil." For a deeper relationship with our Father, we must resolutely repent of our sins and must be washed clean with the blood of Jesus Christ. Why? Because the Father is righteous.

THE IMAGE OF THE FATHER

After reading about the God of Abraham, Isaac and Jacob and our good and righteous Father, what image do you have of Him? How do you see God?

THE ANSWER TO THE PROBLEM

Upon leaving Judea and heading for Galilee, Jesus passed through Samaria. There He met a woman by a well. She had had five previous husbands and was now living with her sixth husband. Her life had not been easy, and she was tired of life. She thirsted for something that could quench her thirst and bring peace of mind, something yet unknown to her.

Jesus spoke to her, "Everyone who drinks this water will be thirsty again, but whoever drinks the water I give him will never thirst. Indeed, the water I give him will become in him a spring of water welling up to eternal life" (John 4:13–14).

Having met Jesus, the woman was able to quench her spiritual thirst, and the water of life sprang forth within her heart. The woman threw aside her bucket and ran to town to witness the miracle of Jesus Christ.

Through this woman, we see that God is the one who provides the answer to our deep-rooted problem. The deep-rooted problem that all people face is original sin. Paul wrote, "For all have sinned and fall short of the glory of God" (Rom. 3:23).

All of us have spiritual lacking—a thirst—like the Samaritan woman, and we cannot quench the thirst ourselves. Jesus Christ knew well of the spiritual thirst of every man. As the thirst could not be quenched by anything of this world, Jesus did not condemn the woman for her sinful living, but instead, He offered her the solution for the quenching and the redemption of her spirit. God our Father desires to forgive and save us.

THE CURE FOR HOPELESSNESS

After Adam's fall in the Garden of Eden, man's body and soul began suffering from a fatal disease. Due to the broken relationship with the Father, man's body and spirit no longer existed in unison. This led to the unavoidable diseased condition of man.

People groan from the pain of various kinds of diseases. In addition to the diseases of the body, people suffer from diseases of the mind caused by guilt of the original sin, a loss of purpose, a sense of futility and the fear of death. Man suffers without hope. For those of us living today, the most important thing is to find the cure.

Who can cure us from such hopelessness and discord? That person is Jesus Christ. He came into this world from God the Father to proclaim the Good News. He healed many suffering ills, and then He died on the cross to redeem us from sin and to resolve the discord between our bodies and spirits. If anyone should come to Jesus, He will heal him of all his ills.

While in this world, Jesus Christ was invited to a wedding feast in Cana. With the feast well under way, the master of the house ran out of wine. This was a serious situation for the bride and groom who were starting out on a new life. Jesus changed water into wine and provided a solution to the problem.

This was the first miracle performed by Christ while here on earth (John 2:1–11). Why did Jesus Christ choose changing the water to wine as His first miracle? One reason was to show us the importance of the institution of families and to show that God transforms our environment as well as our destinies.

THE RESTORER OF RELATIONSHIPS

Between a father and his son, there is an unbreakable relationship. No matter how homely or deformed that child may be, the father looks upon his child with love and considers the child precious. If love and care exist between an earthly father and his physical son, how much greater is our heavenly Father's love for His children?

While there is absolutely no place for sin where the Father is concerned, and although He cannot tolerate sin, He does have pity toward sinners. What is the evidence of this? He has sent His Son to bear the cross for sinners. As a result, any person who repents is forgiven of his sins. But for those who refuse to accept Jesus Christ and His immeasurable grace, the only choice left is to receive the Father's anger and judgment.

Jesus Christ cried as death approached Him, "My God, my God, why have you forsaken me?" (Mark 15:34). Jesus Christ was not tainted with sin, but to purchase our redemption, He was harshly judged (2 Cor. 5:21).

After His resurrection, Jesus Christ appeared before Mary Magdalene and made a request. "Go instead to my brothers and tell them, 'I am returning to my Father and your Father, to my God and your God'" (John 20:17).

God has become our Father through the power of redemption and the resurrection of Jesus Christ.

To all who received him, to those who
believed in his name, he gave the right to

8

become children of God—children born not of
natural descent, nor of human decision or a
husband's will, but born of God.
—JOHN 1:12–13

As such, there is an unbreakable relationship between God and us. God has forgiven us of our sins and has made us His children. He then works to transform the very environment we live in and to bring us a blessed destiny.

THE ETERNAL GOD

I was on the verge of death at the age of seventeen from lung disease. My future was without promise. As I stood at the crossroads of life and death, I came to reflect on the existence of God. "If God did really exist, where is He now? Can He save even me? What does God do anyway?"

Just then, a Christian sister led me to church, and I began to read the Bible for the first time in my life. The Word and the supernatural miracles overwhelmed me and left me speechless. I met God through the Bible, and I received all the answers to my problems and a new life as a gift from God.

When we pray, "Our Father in heaven," we may come to think that God only resides high up in the sky somewhere. However, when we look at the Book of Genesis, we know that our first ancestors, Adam and Eve, dwelled in the Garden of Eden and associated with God freely. But after the sin of disobedience, man could no longer associate freely with God. So now, how can we meet God face to face today, associate with Him freely and live in obedience?

GOD IN THE OLD TESTAMENT

In the Old Testament, God met the prophets at places and through methods ordained by Him. For example, Israel communicated with God by sacrificing the blood of some designated animal on the altar. During the forty years of the

Exodus, the Israelites communed with God through the "veiled" altar. God commanded Moses to build the altar in the tabernacle, gave the Israelites the Law and communed with them.

After the days of Solomon, Israelites could meet with God in the temple. They went to the temple of Jerusalem and worshiped the Lord, asking for compassion and grace. But as the people of Judea began to worship idols, God judged them— and the temple of Jerusalem was destroyed by the Babylonians in 586 B.C.

The Israelites were slaves to the Babylonians for seventy years, and upon their return to Jerusalem, they rebuilt the temple and began a movement to reawaken their faith. However, that was short-lived, and it failed. God broke the resultant four hundred years of darkness that fell on the Israelites by sending them the promised Messiah.

GOD IN THE NEW TESTAMENT

In the New Testament, God communes with us through Jesus Christ. Christ said, "I and the Father are one" and "Anyone who has seen me has seen the Father" (John 10:30; 14:9). Christ, who is the Son of God, is the way we meet God. To know Jesus is to know God.

The meeting places of God in the Old Testament were the altar, the tabernacle and the temple. These were models and shadows of Jesus Christ. They foreshadowed Jesus Christ who came in the physical body of a man to bear the cross for humanity and wash away the original sin of man. As prophesied in the Old Testament, Jesus Christ died on the cross and was resurrected in three days.

GOD IN THE MODERN AGE

Today, the God of the Trinity still moves and does His work through the Holy Spirit. Many people believe God no longer involves Himself in today's world but has become a mere conceptual being. However, God rules the history of mankind. He keeps His covenants, and He continues to guide mankind through them.

In John 5:17, Jesus said, "My Father is always at his work to this very day, and I, too, am working." God of the Old Testament who divided the Red Sea is the same God today who continues to work beside us.

The religious reformer Martin Luther became greatly disappointed and discouraged. His wife, seeing his disappointment, wore a funeral dress and told him, "Dear husband, the Lord God is dead."

Martin Luther, hearing these words, said to her, "What blasphemous words are those? The eternal God is dead? You should not speak such words even in jest."

His wife then replied, "Then why are you so disappointed and discouraged as if God was dead and no longer exists?" Martin Luther then realized his wife's intent and began his work for God with renewed strength.

At times, all of us are also disappointed and discouraged. One of the reasons for such a state of mind is because we doubt God and His presence among us. As long as we believe in Him, there is no reason for us to doubt Him or His love. Such hope constantly reminds us of the Father's love for His children.

And so we know and rely on the love God has for us. God is love. Whoever lives in love lives in God, and God in him.

—1 JOHN 4:16

God who loves us today makes His presence known through the Holy Spirit and works among us in this way. We should not worry about anything at all, but believe in God and depend on Him. The Father prepares the way for His children and makes His presence known through the Holy Spirit. We must live our lives in accordance with His will, knowing that He is at work among us.

Omnipotent Father, thank You for showing us Your goodness and righteousness. Thank You that You work in cooperation with us to fulfill Your will. Help us to truly know You so that we may have in-depth communication with You. Allow us a confident faith, and help us live as Your children. O wise and gracious God, we want to experience Your life among us even today. Help us to look toward You with burning desires of the heart and mind. In Christ's name, amen.

TWO

The Ways of the Father

God has a plan for the world and all things in it. He also has plans for each individual. Accordingly, we must become sensitive to God's voice so that we may hear and follow His will and commands.

GOING GOD'S WAY

In order to walk down the path God has prepared for us, we must first tune our ears in order to hear His voice. The Israelites had lived as slaves for four hundred thirty years in Egypt. They heard the voice of God through Moses telling them the path to follow. The God of Abraham, Isaac and Jacob told them that He would be glorified by leading them into the Promised Land of Canaan, a land where milk and honey ran in abundance.

However, the Israelites lost sight of God's plan, and when their journey became difficult, they grumbled and asked to go back to Egypt. When God spoke through Moses, they hardened their hearts and disobeyed God's will. As the writer to the Hebrew Christians said:

So, as the Holy Spirit says: "Today, if you hear
his voice, do not harden your hearts as you did
in the rebellion, during the time of testing in
the desert, where your fathers tested and tried
me and for forty years saw what I did. That is
why I was angry with that generation, and I
said, 'Their hearts are always going astray, and
they have not known my ways.'"
—Hebrews 3:7–10

The Israelites hardened their hearts, chose to ignore God's way and turned their ears away from Him. As a result, God let the Israelites go their own way.

The Bible shows us God's way. The psalmist wrote, "Your eyes saw my unformed body. All the days ordained for me were written in your book before one of them came to be" (Ps. 139:16). God has plans for each one of us. We must realize that God has planned our lives to the fullest and has prepared a path for us to follow. Then, we must turn our ears to the Lord.

How can we hear and distinguish His voice? That is the work of the Holy Spirit. The Holy Spirit helps us to recognize and see the path the Father has prepared for us. God has spoken through Moses and various other prophets to lead us through the Holy Spirit. We must always trust and depend on the Holy Spirit, tune our ears to His voice and follow His commands.

Finding God's path

In order to know and follow God's path, we must depend on His voice. We must search for His path with all of our hearts. Many people decide on the path they desire to follow, and then they ask for God's help. Rather than following God's will, they struggle to persuade God to help them in their own endeavors. But in God's eyes, this is the wrong path. This is like a person making himself the master of his life and delegating the position of second fiddle to God.

Some have found the path prepared by God, but they refuse to follow it. Paul wrote to Timothy, "For Demas, because he loved this world, has deserted me and has gone to Thessalonica. Crescens has gone to Galatia, and Titus to Dalmatia" (2 Tim. 4:10). If we abandon God's path because of hardship and follow the path of worldly desires, God will not go with us. For those of us who have found God's path, we must not be swayed to the right or to the left, but we must follow the path to its end.

Although we may not see any proof with our eyes, hear with our ears or feel with our senses, we must believe that the road God has chosen is the quickest and the best road to follow.

By relying on the Bible we can fully realize where that path lies. When we listen, read or meditate on God's voice, the Holy Spirit helps us by stirring up greater desires to learn even more. Then, the Spirit opens our eyes wide and brings about a clear focus and realization. We may not know the path now, but when we pray and wait, we will come to see clearly the path we must take.

Before this realization comes, waiting is the proper thing to do. If we do not wait, but try to start down a road before God has that road prepared for us, we will face hardships. If we wait for the Lord to show us the way, God will show us the path He has chosen. David was able to proclaim, "Your word is a lamp to my feet, and a light for my path" (Ps. 119:105).

FOLLOWING THE PATH

Once we find the path, we must follow it in faith and obedience. "And to whom did God swear that they would never enter his rest if not to those who disobeyed? So we see that they were not able to enter, because of their unbelief" (Heb. 3:18–19).

The reason that the Israelites could not enter Canaan was because they did not believe or obey the Lord. The only proper way to follow God's path is through complete faith and obedience.

Being faithful is waiting patiently for God to act. Just as Abraham waited patiently for God's miracle, we must have faith and wait patiently for God to work His miracles in our lives.

As it is written: "I have made you a father of many nations." He is our father in the sight of God, in whom he believed—the God who gives life to the dead and calls things that are not as though they were.
—ROMANS 4:17

Although it may seem impossible to our human minds, we must have faith in the Lord who can create something from nothing. "But my righteous one will live by faith. And if he shrinks back, I will not be pleased with him" (Heb. 10:38).

God has made plans for each of us even before we were born. We must realize these plans through the Word and prayer, and we must follow the path in faith and obedience. To help us do so, let's look at God's will and His ways as shown in the Bible.

GOD'S WILL AND CREATION

When we look at the universe, we can see God's will as it is revealed in Genesis.

THE FIRST DAY

When God created the world, He first created the "light." The light represents hope, life and success. But more importantly, the light is symbolic of Jesus Christ. Jesus Christ bled for us on the cross, and He has brought us out from the dark powers of sin to the light of salvation. In the beginning, God said, "Let there be light" (Gen. 1:3). God also tells the people who are suppressed by Satan to "come to the light." If we accept the light that is Jesus Christ, we shall be transported to the kingdom of heaven where eternal life and light reign.

THE SECOND DAY

God made the firmament and divided the water under and above the firmament. He "called the firmament Heaven" (Gen. 1:8, KJV). For man there is yet another "heaven" to which Christians go after death. However, the Fall of Adam and Eve had closed the gates of heaven. Man became a tragic being in the darkness of despair without knowledge of where he came from, why he lives and where he is going. When we confess our sins and accept Jesus into our hearts, our spirits find life and communication with God. The gates of heaven are opened, and we reside in the kingdom of God even while living in this world.

THE THIRD DAY

God gathered the water and let dry land appear. God called the body of water "sea," and He called the dry land "earth" (Gen. 1:9). He also brought forth grass, vegetables and fruits from the earth. Today, God establishes dry land upon which we can stand in this world of confusion where moral principles and ethics have been lost. That dry ground is the "salvation of the cross." We used to live amid the confusion of the world. Through faith in Jesus Christ, we have found solid ground upon which we can stand.

As we depend on the cross of Jesus Christ, we have become like branches on the tree of life. We must bear fruit that pleases God, the fruit of the Holy Spirit: love, joy, peace, patience, kindness, goodness, faithfulness, gentleness and self-control. (See Galatians 5:22–23.) We must ask the Holy Spirit to help us bear these fruit. We must realize that bearing such fruit requires us to obey God's commands. Only through our earnest prayers and full obedience can we bear the fruit of the Holy Spirit.

THE FOURTH DAY

God created the sun, moon and stars, and divided the day and night, the seasons and the years (Gen. 1:14–18). Just as God created the sun, stars and moon to put order in the universe, God desires us to live within a certain order. Furthermore, God wants us to be filled with wisdom, intelligence, faith, hope and love just as the sky is filled with the sun, moon and stars. God who created the universe desires that we have spiritual orderliness, wisdom and intelligence. We must pray to God for wisdom and intelligence, asking that He grant us the faith, hope and love that is reflective of Christ's life.

THE FIFTH DAY

God created the birds in the sky and the fish in the water. He told all of life to "be fruitful and increase in number" (Gen. 1:22). When we look at God on the fifth day of Creation, He fills all things and places with good things that have life, and He makes them abundant. People claim that living a destitute life is the will of God; they think that living in destitution is true faith. They say that because Jesus lived in poverty, we must live in poverty as well. This is contrary to the will of God, who blesses all things. God blessed the birds in the sky and the fish in the sea. "Be fruitful, and multiply" (KJV) are words of blessing from God. Other than living in self-imposed modesty for the purpose of spreading the gospel, we must be abundant in all things in order to do God's work. We must ask for abundance in all things, and being thusly blessed, we must work for God and His will.

THE SIXTH DAY

God created Adam and Eve in His own image and told them, "Be fruitful and increase in number; fill the earth and subdue it. Rule over the fish of the sea and the birds of the air and over every living creature that moves on the ground" (Gen. 1:28). God's creation of man in the image of the Trinity implies that He created us with the attributes of spirit, body and moral conscience. Adam and Eve were deceived by Satan, who caused them to disobey God's command and lose the image of God.

The eternal curse engulfed all of us. Having lost the image of God and not being able to communicate with God, Adam and Eve were destined to pass to all their descendants the corrupt fruits of sin. However, if we accept Jesus Christ as our Savior and place Him at the center of our lives, we regain that which Adam and Eve lost. God leads us to salvation and renews us so that we can rule over our world in the name of Jesus Christ. If we believe in Jesus and embrace God who has created the world and provides all things, we shall find eternal rest as well as eternal life. God our Father desires that all things in our lives be made well just as He made our souls well. And having received new life from Him, He is pleased when we live our lives in full blessing.

GOD'S WILL AND THE TEN COMMANDMENTS

Every nation on earth has established laws in the form of some constitution. For those of faith, there are laws that serve to guide us. Originally, the Ten Commandments were given to the Israelites through Moses. They exist today as laws for all Christians to obey.

THE FIRST COMMANDMENT

You shall have no other gods before me.
—Exodus 20:3

The creator of the world is God. However, the fallen angel Lucifer and the other angels who followed him have become the false gods on earth, and they confuse people and lead them to worship many gods.

Just as every person has only one biological father, so we must worship our one and only Father God. We must believe and worship only God who is the Father of us all. If we disregard God and worship other gods or other men in place of God, we are sure to be forsaken by the one God.

THE SECOND COMMANDMENT

You shall not make for yourself an idol . . . You shall not bow down to them or worship them.
—Exodus 20:4–5

God commands us not to make any idol and not to worship idols. If we make images and statues as a work of art rather than to worship as idol, we have not sinned. However, if we make an image resembling a certain thing and we bow and worship it, God has promised to punish three to four generations of the household (Exod. 20:5). We must denounce all form of idol worship and obey God's commandments. When we do so, we shall be blessed to thousands of generations (v. 6).

THE THIRD COMMANDMENT

You shall not misuse the name of the LORD your God.
—Exodus 20:7

Misuse of God's name is using God's name for the purpose of ridicule or jest. If a person were to use his father's name in vain or in ridicule, he would be called an "unfaithful son," be condemned by others and receive his father's wrath. Likewise, should a person misuse the name of God the Father, that person cannot possibly escape God's wrath. We must always respect God's holy name and never use His name in vain.

THE FOURTH COMMANDMENT

Remember the Sabbath day by keeping it holy.
—Exodus 20:8

The Sabbath is Saturday, but in modern Christianity, we

observe the Sabbath on Sunday. The Sabbath is the day God has chosen and blessed, and it is the day on which Christians worship God and glorify Him. It is also the day we do work related to the gospel and focus our devotion on the Lord. Other than doing what is absolutely necessary for maintaining our lives, we must not do any work of a personal nature. We must abstain from anything related to pleasure and only devote ourselves to God on the Sabbath.

THE FIFTH COMMANDMENT

Honor your father and your mother.
—Exodus 20:12

Honoring our parents not only means respecting them, but also not becoming the source of worries and concerns for them. This is the first commandment of God that is associated with His blessing (Eph. 6:2). When we live in thanks and respect for our physical parents, not only is God pleased, but He also bestows upon us blessings of success and fruitfulness.

THE SIXTH COMMANDMENT

You shall not murder.
—Exodus 20:13

Our lives were made in the image of God and are subject to God. Therefore, a man who is a creation of God cannot overstep God's authority and take the life of another. The destruction of life, whether suicide or homicide, is a sin. We must honor the lives of others.

THE SEVENTH COMMANDMENT

You shall not commit adultery.
—Exodus 20:14

Adultery is a sin that defiles one's own body. The apostle Paul wrote, "Flee from sexual immorality. All other sins a man commits are outside his body, but he who sins sexually sins against his own body" (1 Cor. 6:18). The writer to the Hebrews said, "Marriage should be honored by all, and the marriage bed kept pure, for God will judge the adulterer and all the sexually immoral" (Heb. 13:4).

Today, numerous families are broken because of sexual immorality and adultery. In order to protect us from this tragedy and keep a happy family, we must flee from adultery and sexual immorality and maintain a life of holiness and purity.

THE EIGHTH COMMANDMENT

You shall not steal.
—Exodus 20:15

Amassing property and wealth through hard work and labor is meritorious. However, obtaining wealth and property without working or through some illegal means is a sin. Just as your property is dear and valuable to you, so is the property of others to them. We must work hard to obtain our own possessions, and we must use those possessions to glorify God.

THE NINTH COMMANDMENT

You shall not give false testimony against your neighbor.
—Exodus 20:16

In this world where morality has deteriorated, lawsuits against one's neighbors abound. Whether through jealousy or incitement by another, there is nothing more evil than bearing false witness against our neighbors. Christians should never commit this sin of false witness that can destroy society as well as our relationships with our fellow man. We should only speak the truth (Eph. 4:25).

THE TENTH COMMANDMENT

**You shall not covet your neighbor's
house . . . or anything that belongs to your
neighbor.**
–EXODUS 20:17

The Bible states that coveting the wife or property of your neighbor is a grave sin. Coveting refers to having greed for things beyond your capacity to own. In a way, this is similar to worshiping false idols (Col. 3:5). This is because those who covet are slaves to the idolatry of coveting. A person who is filled with a covetous heart cannot be used by God. We must give thanks for what we have and be satisfied (Phil. 4:11; 1 Thess. 5:18).

Although we have been saved through the grace of Christ Jesus, we must look upon our lives through God's Word. The Ten Commandments are laws given to us by God to serve as a mirror and guide, helping to show us the things that God hates as well as showing us the way He leads.

THINGS GOD DESPISES

Our enemy the devil tries to lead us down the path of a corrupt body at every opportunity. For example, throughout the history of Israel there are incidents of the Israelites being condemned by God because they fell victim to Satan's scheme and indulged in the desires of the flesh. What are the desires of the flesh that God hates?

IDOL WORSHIP

After coming out of Egypt and starting on their journey to the Promised Land, the Israelites arrived at the foot of Mount Sinai. Moses went up Mount Sinai for forty days to wait for God to give the Israelites the Ten Commandments. (See Exodus 24:18; 31:18.)

The waiting became long and drawn out. The Israelites

became impatient and went to Aaron and asked him to "make us gods who will go before us" (Exod. 32:1). Aaron collected all the gold that the people had and made an image of a calf. He then proclaimed the image of the calf as the "gods, O Israel, who brought you up out of Egypt" (v. 4). The Israelites feasted with food, wine and dance in worship of the idol.

As the feast was well under way, Moses came down from the mountain with the Ten Commandments written on two tablets. He was greatly angered by what he saw. In his anger, Moses threw down the two tablets and broke them. He took the golden image of the calf and burned and ground it into powder. He then mixed the powder with water and made the Israelites drink the water. God then destroyed those who participated in the worship of the idol. (See Exodus 32:13–28.)

Today, Christians say, "We do not worship any golden calf or any idol made of wood for that matter." However, the apostle Paul wrote to the Ephesian church that anyone who lusts after anything is an idolater. (See Ephesians 5:5.) Just because Christians do not have some image of an idol that they worship does not mean that they do not worship idols. If we have anything in our hearts that we love more than we love God, we are worshiping an idol.

To guard against idol worship, we must constantly examine ourselves to see whether we love money or fleshly pleasures more than we love God. We must seek His kingdom and live a God-centered life.

ADULTERY

There is the record of the Israelites being judged by God due to their adultery in Numbers 25. While the Israelites were in Shittim, they attended the idol worship services of the Moabites, bowed to their idols and indulged in sexual immorality with Moabite women. God was angry with those who committed such adultery, both physically and spiritually.

He told Moses to round up all the chiefs of those who participated in the defilement and "kill them . . . in broad daylight" (v. 4). God also unleashed a contagious disease and destroyed twenty-four thousand of His people.

Today, many families are being destroyed because of sexual immorality in a society where lewdness and dissipation is rampant. We must abstain from committing adultery of the soul as well as the sexual immorality of the body.

TESTING GOD

Satan approaches us and tests us by throwing us a question: "Is God really with you?" Despite the fact that God does indeed reside in our hearts, we sometimes doubt His presence. God despises our doubt.

While living in the desert, the Israelites did not fully believe and depend on God. They were afraid of their enemies, and they endlessly tested God for food and water. In the end, they were forsaken by God.

Jesus was also tested by Satan in the desert.

"If you are the Son of God," he [Satan] said, "throw yourself down. For it is written: 'He will command his angels concerning you, and they will lift you up in their hands, so that you will not strike your foot against a stone.'"
–MATTHEW 4:6–7

Jesus overcame Satan's temptation. And so can we.

Testing God is an absolute contradiction. God is not an object of our curiosity or our doubts. He is our Father whom we must respect with all our hearts.

And now, O Israel, what does the LORD your God ask of you but to fear the LORD your God, to walk in all his ways, to love him, to serve the LORD your God with all your heart and with all your soul, and to observe the LORD's

commands and decrees that I am giving you
today for your own good?
—DEUTERONOMY 10:12–13

RESENTING THE LORD

The Israelites could not enter Canaan where milk and
honey flowed even though it lay right before their eyes.
Rather they perished while they wandered in the desert for
forty years (Num. 14:1–45). The Israelites did not know how
to give thanks to God. They grumbled and resented their
God.

Even today, resentment and complaints not only harm
our physical health, but they also destroy many other aspects
of our lives. No matter what situations we are in, we must
live with thanks to God.

Some people view all things with resentment and lamen-
tation, and thereby ruin themselves. On the other hand,
some people view all things positively, and by giving thanks
continually, they turn even their hardships into opportunities of God's grace and blessings. We must learn to turn the
hardships that confront us into opportunities of blessing.

Satan tries to destroy us by tempting us to do those things
that God despises. We must always firmly overcome Satan's
temptation with a strong faith and trust in God.

*O living God, even today our enemy the devil
continues to look for opportunities to destroy our
souls by tempting us with the ways of the flesh,
ways that You hate. Send Your Holy Spirit to help
us follow our path through prayer, faith and the
Word. Help us to overcome these temptations with
the power of the Spirit, and help us to live Christ-
centered lives. In Jesus' name, amen.*

THREE

The Authority of the Father

Christians are those who have decided to live under the Father's watchful eyes and under His authority. When we look upon the world with God's eyes, we can lead successful lives of faith. However, for us to live in and look upon this world through His perspective and under His authority, we must first examine whom God considers as righteous.

JONAH AND THE NINEVITES

God commanded Jonah to spread the warning of judgment at Nineveh (Jon. 1:2). But, thinking Nineveh had persecuted the people of Israel and thus was an enemy of the Israelites, Jonah disobeyed God's command and boarded a ship headed for Tarshish.

However, because God saw Nineveh with the purpose of salvation, He sent a great wind to the ship. The sailors on board the ship were greatly frightened and decided to single out the person who was responsible for the mighty storm. To do so, they cast lots, and Jonah was selected. To appease the storm, Jonah was thrown overboard and was swallowed up by a great fish.

While in the fish Jonah acknowledged and repented of his disobedience. He repented of not having seen things through God's perspective. He also decided to live his life in obedience to God's purposes, not according to his own human perspective. The Lord heard his prayer and caused the great fish to heave Jonah up onto a beach. Jonah, whose survival of the ordeal was nothing less than a miracle, went to Nineveh to proclaim, "Forty more days and Nineveh will be overturned" (Jon. 3:4).

The king and the people of Nineveh, having heard the warning, came forth to God, wearing sackcloth, sitting in ashes and fasting and repenting of their ways. Thus, they escaped the judgment of the Lord.

We also face the dilemma of having to decide whether to follow our human wisdom and perspective or placing our trust in God's ways. At such times we must abandon our human ideas and precepts and wholly accept God's. Only then will God work in and through us.

ABRAM

By examining Abram's life, we can learn more about how faith requires us to abandon our own point of view and take on God's point of view.

Abram received God's command to "leave your country, your people and your father's household and go to the land I will show you" (Gen. 12:1). Upon hearing God's command, which included a promise to make a great nation through him, Abram left Haran at the age of seventy-five (vv. 2–4). After a considerable time, he was still without a son. Then God spoke to Abram again and confirmed that his own descendants would become countless. Commanding Abram to look upon the stars in the sky, God promised him that his descendants would be as numerous as the stars in the sky (Gen. 15:1–5).

At this point, Abram stood at the crossroads. Would he follow his own judgment, or would he wholly trust in God? For Abram to put faith in God's words, he needed to truly believe in God. Being faced with such a dilemma, Abram put his faith in God's unfailing words and God considered him "righteous" (v. 6). When Abraham (God changed his name from Abram to Abraham) was one hundred years old and Sarah was ninety, ages at which conception was quite impossible, God bestowed Isaac on Abraham, according to His earlier promise. (See Genesis 21:1–7.)

God bestows miracles that can bring the dead to life on those people who have abandoned all human perspective and have chosen God's perspective. As such, we must always adopt God's point of view.

How God views Christians must be a matter that concerns us today. The Bible contains a clear record of how God views us. "It is because of him that you are in Christ Jesus, who has become for us wisdom from God—that is, our righteousness, holiness and redemption" (1 Cor. 1:30).

God views all Christians today as wise. The worldly person may reflect his own views and say about a Christian, "That man does not have much education or wealth, and he isn't much to look at." However, in God's eyes, all who have accepted Jesus Christ as Savior are considered wise.

Through the cross, God views Christians as righteous. The instant we accept Jesus Christ, sins of our past, present and future are completely forgiven. Through the blood of Jesus Christ on the cross, our sins were forgiven and we were made righteous. Furthermore, we are holy individuals called by God to obey His will. As such, we must strive to live as holy individuals by obeying His commands.

Christians are wise, righteous and sanctified according to God's point of view. We must shed ourselves of our human perspectives and learn to value ourselves as God values us. As we value ourselves with God's standard of value, we must take pride in our lives and live with confidence. When we look upon the world with a human perspective, we can only feel despair and ruin. However, when we look upon life through God's perspective, we are filled with salvation and hope. And as a result of that, we recognize God's authority in the world today, and in true faith, we acknowledge and surrender to His authority.

GOD'S AUTHORITY

When we repent in the name of Jesus Christ, we are forgiven our sins. However, one of the sins that God does not tolerate is the sin of challenging God's authority.

In Matthew 8, there is a record of Jesus healing the centurion. When Jesus entered Capernaum, a centurion came to Jesus and asked for the healing of his servant who was suffering from palsy. Jesus asked where the centurion lived so He could go to his home and heal the sick servant. The centurion said, "Lord, I am not worthy of Your coming into my house. Only speak the words of healing and the servant shall be well." (See Matthew 8:5–13.)

Jesus heard the centurion and exclaimed, "I have never met anyone with faith as great as this throughout Israel." Christ was astonished because the centurion acknowledged God's authority. The centurion had faith that if Jesus spoke, his servant would be cured.

MAN'S MISERABLE HISTORY

God is the creator of everything in the universe. God made Adam and Eve and allowed them to live in the Garden of Eden where no suffering or pain existed. He warned Adam, "You are free to eat from any tree in the garden; but you must not eat from the tree of the knowledge of good and evil, for when you eat of it you will surely die" (Gen. 2:16–17).

The fruit of the tree of the knowledge of good and evil represented God's authority. The judgment of good and evil rests with God. Man fell into temptation by Satan, who suggested that man would be as God if he ate the forbidden fruit. Being tempted with divinity, man ate of the forbidden fruit and committed the grave sin of challenging God's authority. Because of this rebellious sin, man was driven out from the Garden of Eden.

Man challenged God's authority again by building the Tower of Babel. Man's second attempt also failed as God spread confusion. God diversified the language, resulting in the scattering of mankind over the surface of the earth.

During Christ's time, many priests, experts of the laws, Sadducees and Pharisees endlessly defied Jesus. They did not believe He was the Son of God. In the end, they called out to Pontius Pilate, the Roman governor at the time, for His execution on the cross. This was a direct challenge and disregard of God's will and authority.

God had forsaken the Israelites despite the fact they were His own chosen people. God scattered the Israelites over the face of the earth, making them a nation of people without a country to call their own for nearly two thousand years.

Throughout history, God has shown us that whosoever challenges His authority will be punished. Whosoever believes in Jesus Christ shall receive salvation. Those who oppose Him shall receive God's judgment. We must accept Jesus as our Savior and make Him our Lord.

WHAT ABOUT US TODAY?

Consequently, he who rebels against the authority is rebelling against what God has instituted, and those who do so will bring judgment on themselves.
–ROMANS 13:2

31

God's authority is in the church on earth. The church is not simply a place for Christians to gather. The church is the body of Christ where God's authority resides. Man did not establish this authority; it was established by God. What that means is that although God forgives other sins, God judges those who challenge the authority vested in the church. The church was born at Pentecost. The Holy Spirit built and further developed the church. A direct challenge against the church is a direct challenge against God.

Unbelievers as well as Christians often challenge the church. Through such defiance, we bring about hardships to our own lives as well as for those around us. All Christians should firmly recognize the authority of the church, which is based on God's authority.

The history of man is interspersed with rebellion against God's authority. At such moments in history, man was judged harshly by God because God does not tolerate such rebellion. Because God is filled with both righteousness and love, He sent His only begotten Son into this world so that whosoever should believe in Him shall be forgiven of his sins and receive salvation: "For God so loved the world that he gave his one and only Son, that whoever believes in him shall not perish but have eternal life" (John 3:16).

The cross of Jesus Christ offers the only opportunity of salvation for people living today. God has made Christ the King of kings and Savior of saviors. Those who accept Jesus as their Savior shall receive salvation, but those who do not shall be judged. God is the absolute authority, and those who challenge this authority shall be damned.

GOD'S ADMONISHMENT

Because we as Christians have submitted to God's authority, we accept and obey His words of admonishment and encouragement that benefit and provide for us. What words of admonishment does God give us?

A HOLY, LIVING SACRIFICE

In the Old Testament, the Israelites offered animals by drawing blood, placing the parts of the animal on the altar and burning the parts as a sacrifice. But God said, "Offer your bodies as living sacrifices, holy and pleasing to God" (Rom. 12:1). This does not mean for us to physically kill ourselves as sacrifices. Rather, it means to sacrifice ourselves to God through complete obedience.

Although we believe in Christ and have received salvation, if we do not offer ourselves as living sacrifices with complete submission of our human desires, there is a tendency for our carnality to rear its head. Before long, we are overcome with greed and fleshly desires.

"A dog returns to its vomit," and, "A sow that is washed goes back to her wallowing in the mud."
—2 Peter 2:22

Jesus died on the cross so that we do not again become servants of sin. Because of what Jesus did, we can rely on Him and plead, "Lord, please release me from the harness of sin." When we pray thus, the Holy Spirit cleanses and strengthens us so that we can overcome the desires of the flesh and worldly temptations. But many are not able to completely bring themselves before God and submit to His authority. They obtain wealth and prosperity from unholy lives, and they offer these ill-begotten sacrifices to the Lord.

There are thirteen million Christians in Korea today. But how many fulfill the role as light and salt to the world? Of the many reasons offered for the rampant corruption prevailing in Korea, one of them is the Christians' failure in their role as the light and the salt of the world.

Those who confess faith in Christ and live like those who are of the world cannot be said to be genuine Christians. They disobey God's commandments, and they will not escape God's judgment. For true faith, there must be a synthesis of both moral and ethical consciousness.

Christians must examine themselves thoroughly, and then repent of their sins and turn to Christ. Only after a complete self-examination and repentance can Christians become the light and salt of the world and offer themselves as holy, living sacrifices to the Lord.

God's purpose

Do not conform any longer to the pattern of this world, but be transformed by the renewing of your mind.
—ROMANS 12:2

Why did God command us to set ourselves apart from this world? It is because this world is of the evil one. After the Fall of Adam and Eve, this world was given over to Satan, and humanism became the driving force of life. Satan utilized humanism to drive science and culture to new heights, and mankind became slaves to Satan.

Originally, God gave dominion of the earth to Adam and Eve. However, they were evicted, and after the Fall, the authority over earth was usurped by Satan. As a result, this world has become a place where evil and sin reign. With this knowledge firmly in place, we must never allow ourselves to succumb to the world that is based on secular humanism. We must firmly deny the atheistic world-view of secular humanism and must follow a path of a Jesus-centered life.

We must turn away from our evil generation and keep within us a Spirit-filled mind. We must always remind ourselves that all of our sins have been wiped clean by the cross.

Although man was forsaken by God, we must realize the fact that through the cross of Jesus Christ, communication and harmony with God became possible. Jesus took our shortcomings and infirmities upon Himself and cured us of our own illnesses, thereby allowing us to share in multifaceted blessings. Through Christ's victory over sin and death, we have received eternal life and the right to dwell in heaven with Him.

When we come to the cross and realize such knowledge and wisdom, we are made into new creations and filled with living faith. With faith in Christ's sacrifice, we must revere the Bible and learn to discriminate what is God's good and righteous purpose.

With our hearts cleansed anew, we must recognize God's will. Some people only choose to follow God's will if it brings benefits to them; they choose to follow their own wills when they judge that God's will provides no benefits. Christians should say, "Even if it means some sacrifice on my part, I shall follow God's will." When we live with such determination we are able to be led by the Holy Spirit.

THE MEASURE OF FAITH

God has given faith to each Christian according to the measure appropriate to that person. "For by the grace given me I say to every one of you: Do not think of yourself more highly than you ought, but rather think of yourself with sober judgment, in accordance with the measure of faith God has given you" (Rom. 12:3). If we overextend ourselves beyond what our faith can handle, we may falter. On the other hand, we should not be discouraged by not having enough faith.

All Christians are useful and serve God's function. God the Father builds His kingdom on earth by calling on every Christian to spread the gospel. We must not be lazy. We must continue our efforts to act upon this responsibility for the glory of God. No matter how small our faith may be, it will grow stronger as we act upon it. As this faith grows stronger, we will bear fruit thirty, sixty or one hundred times in abundance. In the Father's eyes, each Christian is a holy offering. God desires all Christians to be renewed and to follow in His will.

Holy Father who is our absolute authority, fill us with Your Spirit so that we may know Your will. Help us to view this world through Your perspective. Thank You for showing us Your purpose through the Holy Spirit. We ask that You help us to live according to Your will. I pray this in the name of Jesus Christ, amen.

FOUR

The Compassion of the Father

Just as parents love their children, God loved the Israelites, His chosen people. However, the Israelites had forsaken this blessing and instead worshiped idols and committed iniquities.

In particular, the leaders and government officials were proud and without compassion as they committed wicked sins in pursuit of various worldly desires. They sacrificed contemptuous offerings and observed appointed days only for appearance. In the case of the priests, their inner corruption was beyond description.

Their iniquities led God to lament, "The ox knows his master, the donkey his owner's manger, but Israel does not know, my people do not understand" (Isa. 1:3).

Through the prophet Isaiah, God warned the Israelites of their sins and of the coming judgment. But because of His unlimited compassion and love, He also urged the Israelites to return to Him by turning away from their sins rather than facing the terrible judgment.

For those of us living today, the question is, "Does God extend His love and compassion to the people of today?"

THE PATH TO FORGIVENESS

God has laid open the path to forgiveness for all people everywhere for all times.

The following story happened in the southern part of America. One night, a middle-aged man came home drunk and had a serious argument with his wife. Unable to contain his anger, he stormed out of their home, slammed the door and started up his car.

The man's three-year-old son had followed after him and was standing behind the car. In a state of blind anger, the man backed his car into his son and killed him. After coming to his senses and realizing what he had done, he could not bear his sense of guilt at having killed his son.

Then one day, as he was wandering aimlessly through the downtown streets, he heard bells ringing from a church. He felt as if the bells were pulling him. He entered the church.

The pastor's sermon was on the mercy of God. However, God's message through the pastor failed to register as the man lowered his head with the thought, *A sinner like me cannot possibly be forgiven.* The message finally penetrated his heart: "Jesus died on the cross for your very sins. God will bestow His mercy only if you repent." Unable to hold back his rising emotion, he finally opened his heart, laid down the heavy burden he had been carrying and cried out in heartfelt repentance. Having found new life, he was filled with immense joy and gratitude to the Lord for His mercy, and he decided to pledge his life to the Lord. He devoted his life to an international Christian youth organization.

Do I take any pleasure in the death of the wicked? declares the Sovereign LORD. Rather, am I not pleased when they turn from their ways and live?

—EZEKIEL 18:23

You are forgiving and good, O Lord, abound-
ing in love to all who call to you.
—PSALM 86:5

Whosoever shall come to the Lord shall be forgiven.

THE EXTENT (LIMIT) OF HIS FORGIVENESS

Some people think that because of the seriousness of their sins, they cannot be forgiven. But God put His only begotten Son on the cross to wash away sin; to whom would He deny this cleansing? David said, "Who forgives all your sins and heals all your diseases" (Ps. 103:3). The psalmist also proclaimed, "Yet he was merciful; he forgave their iniquities and did not destroy them. Time after time he restrained his anger and did not stir up his full wrath" (Ps. 78:38).

Also, the prophet Micah says this about our Father, "You will again have compassion on us; you will tread our sins underfoot and hurl our iniquities into the depths of the sea" (Mic. 7:19). God forgives all sins without exceptions.

King David committed adultery with Bathsheba, the wife of his faithful servant Uriah. In order to hide his sin, he had Uriah killed in a fierce battle. The scheme only compounded David's sin.

However, God sent the prophet Nathan to open King David's eyes to his sinful ways. King David immediately repented without rationalizing or making excuses, and he was forgiven of his terrible sins.

The mercy of Jesus Christ is well documented. Jesus forgave the adulteress who had been caught in the very act of committing the sin of adultery. Also, while on the cross, He forgave the terrible robber beside him when the robber repented.

There is no sin or sinner whose sin is too grave or terrible for forgiveness.

We are all vile sinners who deserve to be forsaken. But

God has bought our souls with the blood of His Son Jesus Christ, and having forgiven all of our sins, He has made us righteous.

There is an exception. God will not forgive our deliberate slander of the Holy Spirit. This is apparent when we look at Matthew 12:31: "And so I tell you, every sin and blasphemy will be forgiven men, but the blasphemy against the Spirit will not be forgiven."

During the Old Testament, anyone who rejected the Law of Moses died without mercy on the testimony of two or three witnesses. Punishment was severe and quick. "How much more severely do you think a man deserves to be punished who has trampled the Son of God under foot, who has treated as an unholy thing the blood of the covenant that sanctified him, and who has insulted the Spirit of grace?" (Heb. 10:29).

The Holy Spirit testifies to the resurrection of Jesus Christ that signifies Christ as the Savior of all the people on earth. If anyone denies the Holy Spirit and blasphemes the Holy Spirit, it is as if he has blasphemed against Jesus Christ and committed the sin of disbelief.

Whoever believes and is baptized will be saved, but whoever does not believe will be condemned.
–MARK 16:16

THE LORD'S INTENT

The intent of the Lord God is to forgive the sins of those who honestly repent and believe in Jesus Christ. "I tell you the truth, whoever hears my word and believes him who sent me has eternal life and will not be condemned; he has crossed over from death to life" (John 5:24). When we accept Jesus Christ as our Savior, our sins are forgiven. Those who truly repent and obey God will receive forgiveness and everlasting life, but those who turn away and do not obey cannot escape God's wrath.

According to John 1:9, "The true light that gives light to every man was coming into the world." As such, when we look upon ourselves in the light of God's Word and see something amiss, we must repent, "O God, I have committed that which You consider sin," and immediately abandon our sins. God takes pity upon us, and our sins shall be forgiven (Prov. 28:13). If we repent of our sins, God offers us salvation. He will make us whiter than snow and whiter than lamb's fleece.

OUR RELATIONSHIP WITH THE FATHER

Having proper relationships with others is extremely important, beginning with our parents who gave birth to us, the teachers who guide our education and the elders who provide us with wisdom. We must teach our children to respect them. All relationships between ourselves and those around us are important.

We live in a society comprised of people. In addition to the social relationships, Christians must acknowledge a relationship with God and develop proper attitudes and postures of faith.

Now we shall examine what attitude a Christian must adopt in order to develop a proper relationship with God by examining David's confession of faith from Psalm 23.

"THE LORD IS MY SHEPHERD . . . " (PS. 23:1–3).

David describes his relationship with God as being like that of a shepherd to his flock: "The LORD is my shepherd, I shall not be in want" (Ps. 23:1). We as Christians are the flock, and we must also confess that God is our shepherd. When we do so, we can understand what David meant when he said that he shall not be in want.

First, our Father, the Good Shepherd, leads the flock to green pastures. A shepherd leading the flock to the green pastures represents the shepherd's intent to provide food and

41

shelter for the flock. In other words, David believed that God would take care of food and shelter.

For Christians today, the green pasture has been prepared under the cross of Jesus Christ. The Good Shepherd, our Lord Jesus Christ, paid for our salvation with His life. Jesus said, "I am the good shepherd. The good shepherd lays down his life for the sheep" (John 10:11). We have not only received salvation through the grace of God and Christ's death, but we have also been cured of our weaknesses and diseases, removing us from the curse so that we can partake in the wonderful blessing that God bestowed on Abraham.

Second, the Good Shepherd leads the flock to a source of water. The "water" for Christians is the cross of Jesus Christ. To redeem sinners, Jesus Christ's hands and feet were nailed to the cross. He shed His blood. Christ's blood brought forth the water of life for Christians. If we repent, Christ fills us with the water of life, which provides faith, hope and love, and frees us from the worries of want and need.

Third, God revives our souls and leads us down the path of righteousness. We fall under the pressure of worries, troubles, anxieties and despair. Through these, our souls are weakened. But if we rely on God who is our Shepherd, the Holy Spirit resuscitates our souls through the Word and prayer.

" . . . I WILL FEAR NO EVIL . . . " (Ps. 23:4).

Although God leads us to the peaceful pastures, He may, at times, lead us through dark and gloomy valleys. At such times it is important for us to place complete faith in God. We may question God as we are led through the valley of death, but to question Him is not the proper attitude. God has absolute authority. The apostle Paul wrote in Romans 8:28, "And we know that in all things God works for the good of those who love him, who have been called according to his purpose." We must hold to this promise, cast aside our fears and believe in God's love for His flock.

With our limited knowledge we cannot possibly know God's vast plans. But there is one fact of which we must be certain. God has planned our ultimate well-being. He plans our well-being in all things by strengthening us through various ordeals. As we are led through the valleys of darkness and death, we must remember that Jesus Christ is by our side. We must have a posture of confidence.

"YOU PREPARE A TABLE BEFORE ME . . . " (PS. 23:5–6).

Even Christians, when they come face to face with those whom they consider their enemies, find it difficult to prevent resentment and hatred from filling their hearts. Should their enemy assault them with frightful force that brings devastation emotionally or physically, they lose all hope and come to resent God. They question why God does not intervene. They may even go so far as to give up their faith in God, believing that God simply does not care. It is at such times that we must be firm even in the face of imminent danger from our enemies, and we must stand upright and keep the proper posture of faith.

When we hold fast to our faith, God unfolds before us a feast. This is the Father's way of showing how much He loves His children in moments of danger. When our enemies try to taunt and destroy us, we must cast aside our negative feelings and attitudes and believe in the feast soon to be given us. God fills our cups with overflowing oil in such moments.

In the Old Testament, only the kings, prophets and priests were anointed, or filled, with oil. Today God fills all Christians with oil through the Holy Spirit and lifts the Christians above their enemies. God fights for His children as long as they stand unwavering in their faith.

Although our enemies hope to make us miserable and even destroy us, the oil of the Holy Spirit helps us to become stronger. Our cups overflow with blessings, and we are able to share this overflowing oil with others. David's confession of faith must become our own confessions of faith. God is our Shepherd and we are His sheep. We shall taste His goodness and mercy all of our lives.

THE FATHER WHO RAISES THE DEAD

God forbade the first man one thing: "You must not eat from the tree of the knowledge of good and evil, for when you eat of it you will surely die" (Gen. 2:17). By disobeying God's one and only command, Adam brought death upon himself and his descendants. All people are born with a "dead" spirit. We are doomed to lives with death looming over us, and finally, we succumb to death itself. No matter how much we try to avoid death, all of us are destined to die. Danish philosopher Kierkegaard said that a man is a being who lives his life with a disease called death. The psalmist said, "The length of our days is seventy years—or eighty, if we have the strength: yet their span is but trouble and sorrow, for they quickly pass, and we fly away" (Ps. 90:10). God rules over life and death, but He sent the Holy Spirit to teach us and make it possible for us to believe in Jesus Christ, resulting in the transformation from death and condemnation to that of resurrection and everlasting life in God.

RESURRECTION OF OUR DEAD SPIRITS

Prior to the Fall, Adam and Eve were molded in the image of God, thus enabling them to commune with Him through their living spirits. But the death of their spirits resulted from their sin, and they lost their ability to communicate with God. Since then, although a person has a living, physical body, his spirit is no longer living; therefore, he cannot know God.

All descendants of Adam have spirits that are dead just like Adam, and although they may see and understand the physical world, they cannot know the world of spirits and God.

The Father, in order to revive our spirits, sent Jesus Christ to the world. Jesus paid for the sins of all men. Whosoever shall accept Jesus as Savior shall have their souls cleansed through the blood of Jesus Christ, and they gain the right to enter the spiritual world that cannot be understood with any amount of worldly knowledge. In addition, we gain peace, happiness, faith, hope and love with the help of the Holy Spirit.

This right to spiritual life is a wonderful gift from God and cannot be compared with any amount of glory, honor or achievement in this world. For those of us whose sins have been washed away and who have been given new lives through Christ's sacrifice, we must glorify and give thanks to God always.

RESURRECTION OF THE DEAD BODY

No matter how much man develops science, life in all its complexity, including immortality, is beyond man's science. In the end, man must die.

God took pity on us and sent His only begotten Son. Through the death and resurrection of that Son, He has provided everlasting life. For Christians, there is everlasting life after our passage from this world. "If only for this life we have hope in Christ, we are to be pitied more than all men" (1 Cor. 15:19).

However, Christ's death on the cross and His resurrection has laid down a path for the resurrection of those who believe in the blood of Jesus Christ. When Christ returns to this world, we can joyfully shout, "Where, O death, is your victory? Where, O death, is your sting? The sting of death is sin, and the power of sin is the law. But thanks be to God! He gives us the victory through our Lord Jesus Christ" (1 Cor. 15:55–57).

MAN OF FAITH AND OBEDIENCE

God does not find pleasure in those who cling stubbornly to

their own will. When we abandon our stubbornness and give ourselves to God, He transforms us to those with faith and obedience. Abraham, the father of faith, also needed to be broken of his stubbornness prior to becoming a man of God.

Abraham experienced bitter destruction and disappointment in times of drought and famine. At one point, he sent his wife to the palace of a king to ensure his survival. Through such an ordeal, God broke Abraham of his ego and transformed his life to one of faith and obedience. As long as our egos continue to dominate us, we cannot experience God's miracles. But with the shattering of our ego, God takes charge of us spiritually. Christians must shatter their ego and only accept God's will and blessing. Through Christ's redemption on the cross, God has given life to us who were destined for death. He shatters our ego and helps us to live in faith and obedience.

OUR FATHER PREPARES THE WAY

We live in a world that is much like a wilderness. We encounter various problems, big and small. When we fail to find solutions to such problems, we are filled with fear and agony. When we do find the solutions, we become confident and are no longer afraid. No matter how difficult our situation and problems, we can face and overcome them without losing hope because we have the knowledge that God has already prepared the solutions.

IN THE DAYS OF THE OLD TESTAMENT

The Bible reveals God as "the One who prepares the way." Prior to the creation of mankind, God created the world and everything in it. He then prepared the Garden of Eden, where destruction and injury did not exist. In the Garden of Eden, Adam and Eve did not need to worry about what to eat, what to wear or what to drink. As long as they believed and obeyed God, they enjoyed a life of blessing.

We can obtain greater understanding of "God who prepares" (*Yahweh*) by examining the Exodus of the Israelites from Egypt. When the Egyptians chased the Israelites to the banks of the Red Sea, there were not any boats to carry them across, nor could they swim across. They despaired.

Amid such despair, Moses held to his faith that God prepares the way for His children. Moses stood before the Israelites and proclaimed, "Do not be afraid. Stand firm and you will see the deliverance the Lord will bring you today" (Exod. 14:13). Moses then spread his arms wide with the staff in hand toward the sea. God split the sea with a great wind and opened before the Israelites dry ground for them to walk across. God provides solutions that are beyond the imagination of man.

After crossing the Red Sea, the Israelites spent the next forty years living in the desert. While in the desert, the Israelites witnessed another wondrous miracle—God provided them with food and water.

How could that many Israelites find enough food? It was possible because God prepared the way. God caused manna and quail to fall from the sky and water to spring forth from rocks. While providing food and water, God led them to the Promised Land of Canaan where milk and honey flowed.

IN THE NEW TESTAMENT PERIOD

The manifestation of the Father's providence and love for His children is the promise of salvation. Since the Fall of Adam and Eve, the spirits of all men died and their physical bodies were destined to die through disease and age. In addition to this curse, men were destined to suffer throughout their lives in an environment choked by thorns and thistles in the form of death, dissolution and hatred.

To save mankind from such suffering, God prepared the path to salvation and sent Jesus Christ. Jesus Christ came into this world to forgive sinners, heal the sick, give hope and comfort to the poor and spread the gospel of God's kingdom.

Christ gave up His own life and paid for our sins, diseases, condemnation and death. Jesus Christ accomplished the salvation of mankind that had been prepared by God for all Christians. If we repent of our sins and accept Jesus Christ as Savior, we shall receive forgiveness, salvation, righteousness, hope and resurrection.

At the wedding feast of Cana, Jesus turned water into wine. Also, at Bethesda Jesus fed a crowd numbering five thousand men, not including the women and children, with five loaves of bread and two fish. After He had fed the crowd, there remained twelve baskets full of bread and fish. Through such records we can see how God prepares the answers to our problems and waits for us to ask for His grace. "He who did not spare His own Son, but gave him up for us all—how will he not also, along with him, graciously give us all things?" (Rom. 8:32).

As believers we are the children of God. We must steadfastly believe in God the Father who prepares the way.

GOD THE FATHER, OUR SHIELD OF PROTECTION

God is full of love, compassion, kindness and mercy. He watches over His children, guides them to victory in battles and takes revenge upon their enemies. When we look at the Old Testament, whenever the Israelites trusted God and obeyed His commands, God always fought for them and kept His promise. God still reigns today and fights for His children.

WHEN HE FIGHTS FOR US

When we know God and love Him, He delivers us from our enemies.

"Because he loves me," says the LORD, "I will
rescue him; I will protect him, for he
acknowledges my name."
—PSALM 91:14

However, for God to rescue and protect us, we must first know God's righteous will and obey Him. Many people pray, "O Lord, be by our side in our battles." This is not a righteous prayer. How can we be certain that the side we fight on is the righteous side in God's eyes? Rather, we ought to pray, "O Lord, help me to stand by Your righteous side and help me to live a life of faith and obedience." When we pray thus, we stand by God's righteous side and He fights for us.

In Psalms 77:20 and 78:52, the children of God are compared to sheep. Sheep do not have horns, sharp teeth or nails. Sheep do not have any means of defense, and they are quite defenseless were it not for their shepherd. If God does not protect us with His power, we cannot defend ourselves. That is why God appears to us as the strong defender and the victorious *Yahweh*.

THE FIGHT FOR HIS CHILDREN

As I mentioned earlier, after four hundred thirty years of slavery in Egypt, the Israelites were freed from slavery and led to the Promised Land. On their way to the Promised Land, they were faced with having to cross the Red Sea. There were no boats or bridges for them to cross. To add to their misery, Pharaoh's army was in hot pursuit to recapture the Israelites. The Israelites began to resent Moses and asked, "Did you bring us out to the desert because there are no graves in Egypt?" Moses prayed to the Lord and said to the people, "Do not be afraid. Stand firm and you will see the deliverance the LORD will bring you today. The Egyptians you see today you will never see again. The LORD will fight for you" (Exod. 14:13–14). This passage clearly tells us that

God fights for His children; He is the *Yahweh* of war.

As Moses raised his staff toward the sea, God caused the waters to split to each side. The Israelites were able to cross the Red Sea to the other side. Pharaoh's army followed the Israelites into the Red Sea. The waters were rejoined, and all the men in Pharaoh's army were drowned.

God still lives and works today to fight for us. We must believe in Him.

VICTORY THROUGH PRAISE

In 2 Chronicles 20 there is the account of an amazing battle. During the reign of Jehoshaphat, the king of Judah, the combined armies of Moab and Ammon displayed their strength throughout the land and came to invade Judah. Judah did not have the ability to oppose an invading army, and the people were afraid.

King Jehoshaphat proclaimed a period of fasting for all the people. As Jehoshaphat and the people cried out to God in the temple grounds, God made His presence known through a Levite among them, Jahaziel. Through Jahaziel, God spoke.

Listen, King Jehoshaphat and all who live in Judah and Jerusalem! This is what the LORD says to you: "Do not be afraid or discouraged because of this vast army. For the battle is not yours, but God's. Tomorrow march out against them. They will be climbing up by the Pass of Ziz, and you will find them at the end of the gorge in the Desert of Jeruel. You will not have to fight this battle. Take up your positions; stand firm and see the deliverance the LORD will give you, O Judah and Jerusalem. Do not be afraid; do not be discouraged. Go out to face them tomorrow, and the LORD will be with you."
—2 CHRONICLES 20:15–17

Yahweh made a promise through one of the prophets that He would fight for them. When people repent and earnestly seek the Lord, God protects them with love and compassion.

After hearing God's promise, Jehoshaphat held a discussion with the people and formed a choir. He placed the choir in front of the army and approached the invading armies, as God had told him to do through the prophet. As soon as the enemies began their charge to attack Jehoshaphat's army, all the people began singing in praise to the Lord.

As soon as the praising began, God caused the enemy's combined armies to fight one another. The armies of Ammon and Moab rose together to destroy and annihilate the army of Seir. Once the army of Seir was slaughtered, they turned on one another and began killing each other. When the people of Judah stepped onto the battlefield, there was nothing but corpses lying around. Through God's miracle, self-confusion and agony were placed upon the enemy, and they were led to their own destruction.

When our enemies set upon us, it is easy for us to become depressed and pessimistic. But in our difficulties, we must sing praises to God with even greater faith. "Yet you are enthroned as the Holy One; you are the praise of Israel" (Ps. 22:3).

To be able to sing praises during the darkest hours of our lives is not easy. But if we do sing praises to the Lord, He hears our praises and reveals His wondrous miracles. Praising the Father invites the Holy Spirit and opens the path for God to show us His glory.

Paul and Silas were arrested for preaching the gospel, taken to prison and beaten. With their hands and feet tied, they were thrown into a prison cell. In the middle of the night they prayed and sang praises to God. Their songs of praise awakened all the prisoners. A great earthquake came, causing the prison doors to open. All the prisoners were freed.

Why does singing praises cause such miracles? Praises

represent faith that places trust in the God of victory even in the direst of situations. Our faith glorifies the omnipotent God.

O omnipotent God, thank You for the mercy shown when You repaired our severed relationship with You by sending Christ to earth. We trust and believe in You, our Shepherd, the leader of our lives and our shield. Help us to live a life of trust and victory in You who fight for us so that we may not despair no matter what our situations might be. In Jesus' name, amen.

FIVE

The Blessings of the Father

In order for us to receive all the blessings the Father has prepared for us, we must first love the Lord. Those who love the Lord must obey and put into practice the words and commands of His Son Jesus Christ. Confessing love for the Lord in words but not believing in Him or living a life according to His will cannot be considered love for God.

In order for us to experience God's prepared grace for us, we must seek for the "vertical answer" rather than the "horizontal answer." The answer does not lie with man and our environment. The answer rests with God, who has authority over mankind, history and life after death.

When you face problems, where do you seek the answers? From others? Your surroundings? God has already prepared the answers for you, and He is waiting for you to come and ask for them. He only requires that you ask. "Ask and it will be given to you; seek and you will find; knock and the door will be opened to you" (Matt. 7:7).

TO RECEIVE THE BLESSINGS PREPARED FOR MEN

In addition, for us to experience all of God's promised blessings, we must be guided by the Holy Spirit. When the Holy Spirit works within us, our desires are stirred as we are filled with realization and confidence. We come to understand the solutions to our problems. Only when we wholly depend on the Holy Spirit does God bestow such grace and blessings upon us. As we live in this world we encounter many problems. But because we believe that God prepares the way for His children, we need not fear.

No eye has seen, no ear has heard, no mind has conceived what God has prepared for those who love him.
–1 CORINTHIANS 2:9

All Christians want to experience God's work and personally "hear" His response to their prayers. However, many fail to understand how God works, and they fail to experience the wondrous workings of the Lord. With that being the case, how does God work in our lives?

THROUGH PRAYER

God works through our prayers. Jesus said, "Ask and it will be given to you; seek and you will find; knock and the door will be opened to you" (Matt. 7:7). He also said, "You may ask me for anything in my name, and I will do it" (John 14:14).

Then what kind of prayers does God answer? When we pray in earnest, God answers our prayers. Whether we pray for the glory of God or for some necessity in our physical lives, we must pray with burning desire. When we pray formally without a burning desire in our hearts, God does not answer. In order to experience God's work, we must have a burning desire.

The Gospel of Luke records that Jesus prayed so earnestly

in Gethsemane that His sweat turned to blood (Luke 22:44). It is said that when a person prays with all his being and in earnest, blood vessels in his body burst and the blood is mixed with sweat. When we pray for the fruition of God's will, it moves God to assist us and to break Satan's hold. God said that He moves in response to our earnest prayers (Eph. 3:20–21). In order to experience God's hand at work, we must always pray in earnest.

THROUGH AGREEMENT

Often Christians say, "Pastor, I pray a great deal to the Lord. I always pray at dawn, I pray in special three-day prayer worship services, I pray overnight, and I even go on retreats to pray. Yet, I still have not received God's answer. I am at a loss as to what to do." I teach them through the Word, "Yes, God does work depending on our prayers, but He also takes into consideration our mental attitudes."

No matter how much we pray, if God deems our vessels not big enough to contain all of His blessings, He does not bestow the blessings on us. The "vessels" in this analogy are our "minds." There must be agreement between what we ask of God and our minds. When asking for success, do not think about failure. When asking for health, do not worry about being ill.

From this very minute, your prayers and your mind must be in agreement. When you pray for salvation of your family, think about how wonderful it will be when your family comes and worships in God's church.

When you pray for health, think about how you will move about and enjoy life as a healthy person. When you pray for success in business, think about how your company will expand. Only then will God answer your prayers.

You must never forget that God's blessing is related to your mind. Although there is no proof to be seen and with the future as dark as the night, always think, "I have received

God's answer; I am healthy, I am able, and I will succeed."

THROUGH ABUNDANCE

Open wide your mouth and I will fill it.
—PSALM 81:10

When God blesses us, He does not merely bless us in the amount we request, but He more than fills our vessels. In Psalm 23:1 David says, "The LORD is my shepherd, I shall not be in want." In verse 5, he declares, "My cup overflows."

Jesus said, "I have come that they may have life, and have it to the full" (John 10:10). God fills the vessels we have prepared through our prayers and minds to overflowing.

God is good. He is our Father. Many people mistakenly think of God as being violent, stingy or fearsome. But if we study the Bible, we cannot deny that God is good.

God created man in His own image and commanded him to conquer and rule (Gen. 1:28). When man disobeyed God and was destined to die an eternal death, God sent Christ Jesus to the world to save man.

Romans 8:32 says, "He who did not spare his own Son, but gave him up for us all—how will he not also, along with him, graciously give us all things?" When we wait with a vessel prepared with our prayers and minds in unison, we can experience the wonderful work of God the Father who fills our vessels to overflowing because He loves His children.

GOD IS LOVE

In everyone's life, one of the most important ingredients is love. A family without love is like a barren desert. Any good deed or act done without love is meaningless. Advice and admonition given without love cannot stir any desire or change within a person.

A family living simply but with great love is much happier than a family living in material abundance without love.

Relationships based on love and understanding grow and strengthen. Good deeds done with love bear much beautiful fruit. "And now these three remain: faith, hope and love. But the greatest of these is love" (1 Cor. 13:13).

Despite the fact that we are sinners, God loves us deeply. "While we were still sinners, Christ died for us" (Rom. 5:8). Who would give away his life for others and die in the place of one's enemy?

Jesus died on the cross. He died to cleanse us. To cure us of our disease of sin, He went under the whip. To give us peace, He received punishment. To give us blessing, He wore the crown of thorns. To make us rich, He became poor. To give us happiness, He drank from the cup of agony and despair.

At this very moment, Jesus calls to all those bearing heavy burdens, "I am the bread of life. He who comes to me will never go hungry, and he who believes in me will never be thirsty" (John 6:35). If we realize the great love of Jesus Christ, our wicked hearts will be broken, and we will be transformed.

EMPTY PLACE FILLED WITH LOVE

Saint Augustine confessed, "All men have an emptiness that only God can fill. Until that emptiness is filled, a person cannot be truly happy." Even though we acquire wealth, status and fame, we cannot achieve complete happiness. The fact that God loves us gives us great strength. We become confident when we keep in mind that God considers us more important than the universe.

There was a man who lived a life of resentment over his miserable condition. He was always pessimistic and ready to criticize and blame others for his misery. At a friend's urging, he became a member of a church. Even at church, he could not abandon his pessimism. The man injured the hearts of other church members.

Then one day he was reading the Bible. His eyes were

opened and he discovered himself. He saw what a miserable person he was. He was ashamed and repented to the Lord. As he prayed, the Holy Spirit filled his heart. He experienced the manifestation of the Holy Spirit, and he thought, *Who am I that God should carry the cross and die on it for me?*

He repented of his pessimistic attitude, and he was filled with a positive attitude and love for his neighbors. God called him to study theology. Today, he is a witness for the gospel of Jesus Christ. What turned his life into one of happiness? The love of God overflowing in his heart.

LOVE FOR OUR NEIGHBORS

We must spread this wonderful love of God to our neighbors as a witness. All of us have the desire to share with others our experiences of being emotionally moved. All of us express and share our gratitude toward someone who has done us favors. It is such sharing and helping others that brings joy and happiness to our lives.

A smile and a warm greeting from a person is a small manifestation of happiness that can be shared. The more we share this happiness, the larger it grows, giving us a sense of worth.

Subsequently, how can we revel in the immense love and joy of Jesus Christ? We must be witnesses of the gospel of Jesus Christ and spread its message far and wide.

If we love only those who love us, we are not much better than those who do not believe God. Jesus said, "Love your enemies and pray for those who persecute you" (Matt. 5:44). The verse tells us that we should love with the love of Jesus Christ. When we love those who have trampled on us and insulted us, God in heaven finds great joy.

If anyone says, "I love God," yet hates his
brother, he is a liar. For anyone who does not
love his brother, whom he has seen, cannot
love God, whom he has not seen. And he has

given us this command: Whoever loves God
must also love his brother.
—1 JOHN 4:20–21

The love of the cross is a love we cannot possibly give or
experience with our mere human hearts. For us to share in and
give the love of the cross, we need the help of the Holy Spirit.
"And hope does not disappoint us, because God has poured
out his love into our hearts by the Holy Spirit, whom he has
given us" (Rom. 5:5). We must fill our hearts with the love
that the Holy Spirit pours into us, and we must share this love
with our neighbors. When we do so, we are availing ourselves
of our Father's blessings.

GOD'S BLESSINGS

Paul prayed to God that Timothy would be blessed. Not long
afterward, Timothy was indeed blessed by God. The meaning
of the name *Timothy* is "reverence toward the Lord."
Although the name Timothy is a specific name for an individual, it is also the name of all Christians who glorify the
Lord. Just as Timothy was blessed for his reverence toward
God, the same blessing is given to all Christians. What blessings does God give to those who are in Christ Jesus?

GRACE

The word *grace* comes from the Greek word *charis*. The
original meaning of the word is "beautiful" and "like as
love." In Christianity the word *charis* represents God's
unmerited favor toward us.

Without this grace, there would be no person who could be
saved. This is because there is not a single man who can be
righteous according to the Law of Moses. Through the merit of
Christ's blood, we are deemed righteous and have become
God's children. We must never be proud or arrogant. "But we
have this treasure in jars of clay to show that this all-surpassing

59

power is from God and not from us" (2 Cor. 4:7).

The implication of the jars of clay is that man is of no value, and only through the power and grace of the Lord can his life become one of great value like treasures in the jars of clay.

Paul spoke of himself as "one abnormally born" (1 Cor. 15:8) and that "by the grace of God I am what I am" (v. 10). The more deeply we understand our weaknesses, the more we realize the strength and magnitude of God.

Those who find happiness in God and who are treasured by Him come to realize the grace of God. Our sins being forgiven, becoming God's children, receiving everlasting life and becoming citizens of heaven were not made possible because we were worthy. We must realize that all these things have become reality because of the grace of God, the unmerited favor of the Father toward us.

COMPASSION

Compassion refers to the heart being able to feel pity. If God did not have compassion, we would not be able to escape judgment for our sins. However, God does not treat us according to His laws, but just as parents have compassion for their children, God has compassion for us.

Although our God is the God of righteousness and judgment, He also looks at us with compassion and forgiveness. He is the God of love and forgiveness. God's compassion is not some abstract concept, but it is a compassion that affects our lives.

Just as we have received compassion, we must also have compassion. Jesus said that those who regard others with compassion are worthy to receive God's compassion. Sometimes people are charitable for their name's sake. True compassion bestows love and concern for others in the name of Jesus Christ without desire for recognition and praise. In Luke 10, there is a parable of a man who was met by a robber on his way to Jerusalem. Who bestowed love and compassion on this man? The one who saved the man's life was neither a religious leader nor a priest. Rather, it was a Samaritan who was regarded with contempt and disdain by the Israelites. The Samaritan helped the man and paid the innkeeper with his own money to take care of the man. (See Luke 10:30–35.)

Today, we enjoy the benefits of cultural developments as a result of economic progress. However, there are still those who suffer hunger, illness and live marginal lives in poverty. We have a responsibility to bestow Jesus' love and compassion on these people.

PEACE

Those who live under God's grace and compassion are able to enjoy the fruit of peace. Man can never enjoy peace as long as he lives in fear of punishment and the sense of guilt for his sins. Only through the blood of Jesus Christ can a peaceful relationship be restored. Sins are cleansed through the blood of Jesus Christ. As a result, we experience God's grace and compassion, which makes it possible for us to have a peaceful existence. Jesus said, "Peace I leave with you; my peace I give you. I do not give to you as the world gives. Do not let your hearts be troubled and do not be afraid" (John 14:27).

The peace of the world is momentary and superficial. Some people are content with obtaining worldly wealth, health, power, homes or cars. But when they lose all these things, their peace and contentment vanish. The peace that Jesus gives is everlasting peace. This peace cannot be lost in any circumstance because it springs from within.

To have such peace, what must we do? Jesus said, "Come to me, all you who are weary and burdened, and I will give you rest" (Matt. 11:28). When we come before Jesus, lay our burdens in front of Him through prayer and live according to His will, we shall receive His peace. When we lay aside our worries as we seek Him in thanksgiving and prayers, our Father God gives us peace that springs from our inner man. Only when we are transplanted from the self-centeredness to the everlasting spring can we lower our roots deeply and firmly in Jesus Christ and fully experience God's greatest blessing: salvation.

SALVATION AND MAN'S EXISTENCE

Man is like a ship sailing on the sea. Not knowing where he comes from or where he is headed, man blindly sails through life. In the end, he sinks to the bottom of the sea.

When Adam and Eve resided in the Garden of Eden, they knew where they came from, why they were on earth and where they were headed. Adam and Eve were made by God and were without fault. They resided in the Garden of Eden and knew their responsibility to take care of all things God had made.

However, they fell into the trap laid by Satan, disobeyed God and ate of the fruit from the tree of the knowledge of good and evil. They were severed from their God. They lost their purpose and were overcome with fear and shame. They hid from God. In such dire circumstance, God called out to Adam, "Adam, Adam, where are you?"

God did not call out to them because He did not know where they were. God wanted them to know that they had lost their original position in the Garden of Eden.

THE FALLEN MAN

When God searched for Adam and Eve, they were hiding. Although the Garden was a place filled with peace and happiness, for Adam and Eve, it was no longer a place of rest and comfort.

What did their Fall mean? First, it meant that mankind would be plagued with sin. Before the Fall, Adam and Eve did not know sin. But as soon as they disobeyed God, they became prisoners of sin and discovered that the shadow of sin loomed over them. As sinners they could not stand before God. Sin severed the relationship between them and God.

Second, the Fall meant that they would become victims of death. When Adam and Eve were made in the image of God, their bodies were not destined to die. When they disobeyed God, the glory of God left them and their bodies became destined to die. God said to fallen Adam, "For dust you are and to dust you will return" (Gen. 3:19).

Third, the Fall meant that mankind would become victims of the curse. Adam and Eve were exiled from the Garden of Eden. As exiles they toiled for survival in a land of thorns and thistles, facing the curse and condemnation.

Fourth, the Fall meant that they would be mired in despair. Having been driven from God's side, Adam and Eve lived with anxiety, fear and despair, without knowledge of where they came from, why they were alive and what their purpose in life was. They doubted God's command, and because they disobeyed Him, they lost their rightful place in the Garden of Eden. They now lived under the shadow of sin, death, curse and despair.

Since that time, man has rallied all his wits and ways to free himself from sin and curse, death and disease, fear and despair. However, all his struggles have failed.

WHO HAS THE SOLUTION?

The real purpose of God's search for Adam was to give him an opportunity to realize his sin and to provide a chance to repent. Rather than taking that opportunity to repent, Adam blamed Eve while Eve blamed the serpent. God didn't kill them outright in anger. He killed an animal and made clothes from its skin. In Adam and Eve's place a sinless animal was killed and made to bleed to death, signifying God's will in having the descendant of the woman become the Savior of humanity (Gen. 3:15). This prophecy was fulfilled two thousand years ago.

Jesus came into this world from the body of the virgin Mary and the Holy Spirit. He gave hope to those living in sin and preached the gospel of heaven. And to redeem man's soul, Jesus died on the cross. God allowed Jesus who was without sin to be crucified so that we can wear the robe of Christ's righteousness.

Through Christ's death, we are able to shed ourselves of the shame of sin and are made righteous, filled with the Spirit and are given the right to happiness and blessings. Also, the thorns and thistles of condemnation and curse that choked us are no longer able to injure us. In addition, God has made it possible for us to become rightful citizens of heaven.

The Christian faith is not a religious understanding of some kind. The Christian faith is the acceptance of Christ's righteousness, eternal life, blessing, the Holy Spirit and heaven. The Christian faith is becoming a new creation with Jesus in our hearts. Whosoever accepts Jesus Christ shall be freed from sin and death, the curse and despair, and shall become a changed person. He shall wear the robe of righteousness and live in happiness with eternal life and hope. A man can only despair when he learns the meaning of his true existence. But the God of love does not abandon him. He has prepared a road to salvation through Jesus Christ.

O God of love and mercy, we thank You for having saved our souls. We want to experience Your wonderful work as You live and work among us today. Help us to be moved by Your love and to share Your love with our neighbors. Help us not to lose sight of Your grace and compassion, but help us to be Your children worthy of much blessing. In Jesus' name, amen.

Part Two
God the Son

SIX

The Gift of the Son

As related earlier, the Garden of Eden was perfect. It was the most beautiful garden and plentiful in all things. But Adam and Eve ate the fruit of the tree of the knowledge of good and evil, which represented God's authority. By eating the fruit, they committed a crime against God. As they were hiding behind the trees in the Garden, God called out, "Adam, where are you?" God searched for Adam and Eve.

Did God, who was omnipotent and omnipresent, call out for Adam because He was unaware of where Adam was? No. After Adam had committed his sin, God called out to Adam to give him time to realize the gravity of his sin.

THE ORIGINAL QUESTION

The question asked by God, "Where are you?", is the same question that He asks all people. If Adam had been able to come forward and answer God, his only response would have been, "God, I am fully aware of my sin of disobedience, and I am burdened by a sense of guilt."

Civilization today has been developing at a tremendous rate. However, the descendants of Adam are in the same miserable state as he was. We hide from God just as Adam hid behind the trees in the Garden of Eden.

Exactly what situation was Adam in? Adam faced despair from his sense of shame and guilt. He hid and later was cursed to suffer the illness and death of his physical body. The spiritual despair was one of eternal turmoil and condemnation. For Adam, there was no hope. Once having disobeyed and not repenting, Adam could no longer enjoy the bounty of the Garden of Eden and his privileged place in it.

He was in complete despair. He had disobeyed God and could not escape. The descendants of Adam have received the same fate. Man has tried to escape from this fate through various religions and the development of science and culture. But no one has been able to find a solution. As a result, man laments, "I am surrounded by sins as well as disease and death. I live in eternal condemnation and despair."

To provide an answer to this despair and condemnation, God came to the world Himself and provided us with the answer. Although no man, whether a politician, philosopher or some great hero, has been able to rescue mankind from his predicament, God took on human flesh and came into the world to provide the perfect and final solution.

CHRIST'S ANSWER

Jesus Christ the Son came to show us the grand design of the Father's plan. Through His death on the cross, Jesus provided the final answer for mankind's suffering from despair.

Jesus was nailed on the cross, and through His blood, He saved mankind. After Adam sinned against God, the question asked by God to all mankind, "Where art thou?", had been unanswerable. Now, Jesus has given us the complete and perfect answer to this question. We are now within the arms of God's blessings. As He spoke the words, "It is finished," on the cross, the answer to the question became complete, and with His resurrection, Jesus proved to us that His answer was the truth.

This blessing of salvation that Jesus has prepared is available to anyone who accepts Christ as Savior. Whosoever should believe in Jesus will be given the blessing of salvation. Having received this blessing, we can answer God's question with confidence.

First, when faced with the question "Where art thou?", we can answer, "I have been freed from my sins and stand among those considered righteous in Jesus Christ. Although I have sinned and was cursed from birth, I have gained righteousness by having repented my sins. I am no longer under the control of Satan, but I am able to stand confidently before God."

Second, when faced with the question "Where art thou?", we can answer, "I share in the happiness that is You, O Lord. Although I have been Your enemy, through the Lord Jesus Christ, I am able to call You Father and share in the blessed relationship." In this way, through Jesus Christ we have found happiness with God and can communicate with Him.

Third, when faced with the question "Where art thou?", we can answer, "I am being healed. Through Jesus Christ, I am going through a spiritual treatment, and I am being filled with righteousness, peace and love. Furthermore, my physical body is being treated so that I am blessed with good health."

Fourth, when faced with the question "Where art thou?", we can answer, "I am a part of Abraham's blessings. I have escaped from the thorns and thistles of condemnation. I have been moved to a life overflowing with milk and honey." Once we accept Jesus Christ, we no longer live with the curse and condemnation.

Fifth, when faced with the question "Where art thou?", we can answer, "I have eternal life. With the help of Jesus

Christ, I have the power of victory over death. I shall enter into heaven."

The apostle Paul said, "Now we know that if the earthly tent we live in is destroyed, we have a building from God, an eternal house in heaven, not built by human hands" (2 Cor. 5:1). This verse provides proof that our refuge has been prepared for us in heaven. We shall live eternally in a place without tears, death and despair.

All these things are gifts that Jesus has given to each of us as the answer to God's question. Through Jesus Christ, we live in forgiveness, righteousness, reconciliation, divine healing, health and eternal life. When asked the question "Where art thou?", we can answer, "I have trusted Jesus Christ. I have been forgiven, and I am safe in the arms of God."

Through what Christ has provided for us—through His precious blood—we can stand confidently and proudly answer our God.

THE POWER OF THE BLOOD

Regardless of who you are, you cannot live eternally. The most important thing is life itself.

All men search for the elixir that can extend life. In the hope of extending life, mankind has developed medicine and medical science. Many religions have come and gone with the hope of providing man with the answer to extending life. However, the Bible tells us that eternal life is in God's hands, and as long as we are bound by sin, death is inevitable. Life on earth is nothing more than a road to death.

To save us from this hopeless condition, God sent Jesus Christ to the world. And by dying on the cross and shedding His blood, Jesus opened the door to salvation. As we look through the Bible, the blood is representative of life, and the shedding of blood is representative of redemption.

For the life of a creature is in the blood, and I

**have given it to you to make atonement for
yourselves on the altar; it is the blood that
makes atonement for one's life.**
—LEVITICUS 17:11

Blood has the ability to cleanse and redeem. God required that when the Israelites offered worship, they sprinkle the blood of the sacrificial animal on the altar. The blood of the sacrificial lamb is the blood of Jesus Christ. Within the blood of Jesus Christ, there is hidden the great power of God.

THE POWER TO
CLEANSE ORIGINAL SIN

Man was originally a spiritual being and was created in the image of God. With man's disobedience, sin entered the world, and along with sin, death came to the world. "For every living soul belongs to me, the father as well as the son—both alike belong to me. The soul who sins is the one who will die" (Ezek. 18:4).

A man who has died because of his sin cannot set himself free no matter how much he may struggle. No matter how much good he does, he cannot budge even an inch away from death.

A man killed another man by mistake. Fearing the punishment that would follow, the man ran away. For many years, the police were not able to apprehend him. With the end of the statute of limitation only a few days away, the police captured him. Many people looked at him and said, "What an unlucky man," but the man said, "Now my heart can finally rest." The weight of a guilty conscience for a man who has committed a crime or sin is heavy and burdensome. A man cannot remove this burden by relying on himself.

How can we be released from this great burden of the guilt of sin? We can be freed through the power of the blood of Jesus Christ. "In him we have redemption through his

71

blood, the forgiveness of sins, in accordance with the riches of God's grace" (Eph. 1:7).

VICTORY OVER SATAN

Satan tempted Adam and Eve to commit the rebellious sin against God. Having succeeded, Satan enslaved mankind. Since then, Satan has engaged in endless attempts to destroy mankind. Jesus said, "Now is the time for judgment on this world; now the prince of this world will be driven out. But I, when I am lifted up from the earth, will draw all men to myself" (John 12:31–32). Revelation 12:11 says, "They overcame him by the blood of the Lamb and by the word of their testimony; they did not love their lives so much as to shrink from death."

The blood that Jesus shed on the cross has cleared all debts of sin for all mankind and crushed Satan's authority. The authority of Satan crumbles under the power of the blood of Jesus Christ.

One day I was praying. All of a sudden, indescribable frustration and depression came over me, preventing me from praying. No matter how much I tried to pray, something continued to grip my heart. Just then, the Holy Spirit told me, "Believe in the blood of Jesus Christ and drive Satan away."

I shouted, "I believe in the power of the blood of Jesus Christ. I command in the name of Jesus Christ: Be gone, you devil, who has brought me fear, inability and nervousness." As soon as I spoke those words, the dark clouds disappeared, and my heart was filled with peace and confidence. I experienced light shining through my heart like the sun that shines down in midday. When we acknowledge the power of the blood of Jesus Christ and confess its power, Satan is defeated.

THE POWER TO BRING HARMONY

God is both love and righteousness. Although God loves all

72

sinners, He does not accept or approve of sin. His love and pity for sinners moved God to provide salvation for us by sending us His only begotten Son. He made Jesus Christ carry the cross and be judged on the cross. "For if, when we were God's enemies, we were reconciled to him through the death of his Son, how much more, having been reconciled, shall we be saved through His life!" (Rom. 5:10). We must not forget the fact that because Jesus Christ shed His blood in our place, we were forgiven of our sins and reconciled with God.

Furthermore, the blood of Jesus Christ has the ability to bring peace between the relationships of men.

All this is from God, who reconciled us to himself through Christ and gave us the ministry of reconciliation: that God was reconciling the world to himself in Christ, not counting men's sins against them. And he has committed to us the message of reconciliation.
–2 CORINTHIANS 5:18–19

We must depend on the blood of Jesus Christ and break down the wall of jealousy, hatred and competition between our neighbors. We must live with compassion and tolerance. When we look upon our neighbors, we shouldn't judge them, but by remembering that they are also loved by God, we should live in harmony with them. The blood of Jesus Christ has the power to cleanse our sins, destroy Satan's power and bring peace with God as well as with others.

Through the precious blood of Christ, we are prepared to become the temple of God—the home of Christ, who dwells within each Christian.

CHRIST IN ME

After Adam and Eve committed sin and were driven out of the Garden of Eden, mankind could no longer have fellowship with God. In this separation our souls died. Even while still in this world, we went down a thorny path. We were caught in Satan's noose. However, God pitied us and planned a sacrificial way for us so that we could be saved. To accomplish this Jesus Christ came into this world.

Jesus Christ, the Son of God, gave up His residence in heaven and came to this earth in a physical body to save mankind. During His ministry, Jesus Christ performed many miracles as He spread His gospel.

Afterward, Jesus Christ endured great suffering and became a sacrificial lamb to die on the cross. He destroyed the power of Satan and of death by being resurrected from the dead. Finally, Jesus Christ ascended to heaven and left behind these words: " . . . teaching them to obey everything I have commanded you. And surely I am with you always, to the very end of the age" (Matt. 28:20). For those of us who live after Christ's ascension, how can we come face to face with Christ and meet Him?

Christians who believe in Jesus Christ do not need to wander in search of idols like the nonbelievers. Why is this? It is because Jesus Christ is in our hearts. Jesus is not in some remote place. He lives within each one of us.

The Bible tells us where Christ resides.

Do you not know that your body is a temple of the Holy Spirit, who is in you, whom you have received from God? You are not your own.
–1 CORINTHIANS 6:19

To them God has chosen to make known among the Gentiles the glorious riches of this mystery, which is Christ in you, the hope of glory.
–COLOSSIANS 1:27

Jesus Christ resides in the form of the Holy Spirit in those who believe and follow Him. He makes His presence known where even two or three people gather in His name.

Although we are foul, ugly and deserve to die an eternal death, if we bow down before Christ, repent and accept Him, we shall receive the blessing of turning our vile bodies into temples of Christ. This blessing disregards the differences of worldly possessions and positions as well as the gender. Whosoever calls on Christ shall be saved, and Christ shall make His residence in the heart of all who trust in Him.

The Bible considers this a "secret" that had been kept for endless time and generations (Col. 1:26). Since the beginning of man's history, many have tried to learn this secret. None has fully grasped and understood it entirely. For the person who accepts Jesus as his Savior, the door that leads to this secret is open. The secret is that our bodies become the temples of the living God (2 Cor. 6:16).

The greatest fact of the Christian faith today is that Jesus Christ resides in the hearts of all who believe. We must always keep our hearts faithful. And by praying and studying the Bible continuously, we fill our hearts with God's blessings.

CHRIST WHO WORKS WITH US

Jesus said, "I tell you the truth, anyone who has faith in me will do what I have been doing. He will do even greater things than these, because I am going to the Father" (John 14:12).

Hebrews 13:8 says, "Jesus Christ is the same yesterday and today and forever." Even after Christ's ascension into heaven, He still works in us in the form of the Holy Spirit.

What is the work that we should be doing? Jesus commanded, "Go into all the world and preach the good news to all creation" (Mark 16:15). Paul urges us, "Preach the Word; be prepared in season and out of season; correct, rebuke and encourage—with great patience and careful instruction" (2 Tim. 4:2). Therefore, we must not be bound and troubled, but we must be diligent in our work of spreading the gospel.

When we faithfully take the action in our ministry of evangelism that Christ commanded, He not only works with us, but He also makes it possible for us to accomplish even greater works. Having understood this truth, we must confidently spread the gospel.

JESUS CHRIST WHO WORKS THROUGH THE HOLY SPIRIT

The Bible says, "And I will ask the Father, and he will give you another Counselor to be with you forever" (John 14:16). Jesus Christ came to earth and did much work two thousand years ago in Israel, and He continues to work among us today through the Holy Spirit.

First, the Holy Spirit assists us in becoming evangelists for the gospel of Christ. Jesus said, "But you will receive power when the Holy Spirit comes on you; and you will be my witnesses in Jerusalem, and in all Judea and Samaria, and to the ends of the earth" (Acts 1:8). The disciples of Christ were able to accomplish their duties of evangelism because they were filled with the Holy Spirit at Pentecost. We must also be filled with the Holy Spirit in order for us to accomplish our duties as a witness for Jesus Christ.

Second, the Holy Spirit makes it possible for us to live in faith. Ephesians 3:16 says, "I pray that out of his glorious riches he may strengthen you with power through his Spirit in your inner being." When we are filled with the Holy Spirit, our faith becomes passionate and bold so that we may live successfully in faith.

When we live by acknowledging, accepting and depending on the Holy Spirit, the Holy Spirit works miracles in our hearts, and as our souls are made well, our lives are made well, and the blessings of living in happiness will overflow. Christ came to the world two thousand years ago to provide for us the miracle of salvation, but Christ's ministry did not end with the ascension of Christ to heaven. Today, Christ works through believers the same way He did when He came to earth.

THE BLESSINGS FOR THOSE IN CHRIST

Believing in Jesus Christ does not come from a person's own volition. Only when God moves on our hearts through the Holy Spirit and opens our hearts can we believe in Jesus Christ. Those of us who believe have received the blessing to be in Jesus Christ.

The Bible says that we are "children born not of natural descent, nor of human decision or a husband's will" (John 1:13). Those who believe in Jesus Christ as their Savior have come to believe through the grace of God. What blessings do Christians receive?

WISDOM OF GREAT VALUE

Those of us who have accepted Jesus Christ as our Savior have within us a wisdom that the unbeliever does not have. That wisdom is the knowledge of where we came from, why we live and where we are headed. This wisdom comes from Jesus Christ who dwells in our hearts. Life that lusts after the flesh is meaningless and empty. A life of following Jesus Christ brings the wisdom to realize that such a life is the only true life.

When we have this wisdom, our spiritual eyes are opened and we can understand the Bible, which brings God's knowledge and power. Although such lives will be viewed as foolish in the eyes of the world, this is the only way to live. The world may not understand why Christians even bother or care, but it is the way to victory and truth. A person who accepts Christ as his Savior will not be condemned. That person will gain the wisdom to live an everlasting life.

RIGHTEOUSNESS

Christians have been declared righteous through the death of Jesus Christ. He cleared all the debts of sin; He is the source of righteousness.

Jesus transforms sinning, immoral and vile people into sinless people in God's eyes. When we receive Jesus as Savior, we are declared by God to be righteous and uninfluenced by Satan. Righteousness is the blessing that awaits each man who accepts Jesus Christ.

HOLINESS TO OVERCOME SIN

The world is filled with sin. Sin cannot be overcome with personal determination or will. Man does not possess the strength to overcome sin. Is man destined to perish forever because of sin? No. The way out is by believing in Jesus, and then by living for Jesus Christ. When we are in Christ, the Holy Spirit causes our hearts to spring forth life-giving water, continually washing us clean of our sins to make us holy.

Even after we accept Jesus Christ as our Savior, we at times suffer emotionally because of some sin we committed and did not repent of. The Holy Spirit encourages us to repent and ask for forgiveness.

THE GIFT OF OUR REDEEMER

Jesus Christ, the Son of God, is the redeemer. Redemption refers to "buying the freedom of a slave with a price." To whom were we slaves, and from what restraints were we freed? We were slaves because of sin. Since the Fall of Adam and Eve, man has been condemned and trapped. We were destined to become a handful of dirt after death.

Jesus Christ became the collateral for our emancipation from sin. By taking unto Himself the condemnation meant for man, Jesus Christ emancipated us. For those in Christ, there is no longer any condemnation. As our spirits are healed and made well, our lives are made well. As we are made healthy, our lives become brighter and happier.

Jesus Christ also became the collateral for healing of our illnesses. The apostle Peter wrote, "He himself bore our sins in his body on the tree, so that we might die to sins and live for righteousness" (1 Pet. 2:24). Matthew 8:17 states, "He took up our infirmities and carried our diseases." In order for Jesus to give us our healing, health and strength, He went under the lashes. He has become a guarantor of life. For Christians death is simply a phase of removing the covering that is our physical body. Once we are removed from our bodily shells, our spirits live with Christ eternally.

Dear God, full of kindness and mercy, we thank You for saving us who were deserving of eternal death. Help us to always depend on the blood of Jesus Christ so that we may lead victorious lives. Let us live lives of victory as we live in harmony with Jesus Christ who dwells in our hearts. While we live in this world, help us to enjoy all of these blessings that come from being one with Jesus Christ. In Christ's name, amen.

SEVEN

The Authority of the Son

In the Old Testament, after God gave His Law to the Israelites, if anyone wished to worship God and give an offering, he needed to see one of the priests. Offering a sacrifice could not be done by anyone. The priests were chosen by God to offer sacrifices. Offering a sacrifice was the right and the responsibility of the priests.

Even among the priests, there was only one high priest who was qualified to enter the holy of holies. In normal times, the high priest represented all Israelites and offered the sacrifices to God.

One of the most important duties for the high priest was to go into the holy of holies once a year to offer a sacrifice for the sins of the whole nation. For such occasions, the high priest had to take the blood of an animal and sprinkle the blood on the altar.

The high priest held the important position of representing the Israelites and offering a sacrifice to God. It was important that this high priest was a man and that he was chosen by God. Neither angels nor any being other than a man could take this responsibility. Only a man who was chosen by God could represent other men and pray for God's forgiveness.

In order to meet this condition, Jesus Christ wore the flesh of a man and came to this world as a man to become the eternal High Priest. How did Jesus Christ become our High Priest?

CHOSEN BY GOD

To be qualified as the high priest, a person must first be called by God. In the Bible, we can see that God had established Aaron as the high priest (Exod. 40:12–15). Regardless of who a person was or how holy he may be, if God did not call that person, he could not become the high priest.

Today, many people volunteer to become a servant of God on their own. To all who come to me for my advice on becoming a servant of God, I ask them a question: "To become a servant of God, there must be a calling by God. Has God called you?"

Then I add, "If there was such a calling, you would not be filled with indecision or doubt about it. You would lose all interest in any other work. You would burn with a desire to become a servant of God." Just as God called Aaron to become the high priest, a person must be called by God to become God's servant even today.

Jesus has become our High Priest through such calling. Hebrews 5:5 says, "So Christ also did not take upon himself the glory of becoming a high priest." This shows us that Jesus did not become the High Priest through His own volition, but He was called by God.

Second, because the high priest must be a person, Jesus came down from heaven's glory to wear a physical body and become a man. Jesus is God. Through the Holy Spirit, He was conceived in the body of Mary. He came into this world and as a perfect man was chosen by God to become the

High Priest who would offer Himself as a sacrifice to God for our salvation.

JESUS OF MELCHIZEDEK'S ORDER

God originally made a covenant with the Israelites and gave the Law. He chose Aaron and his sons to become the priests. All high priests came from this order; whosoever was not of Aaron's order could not become the high priest. All priests, including Aaron, were the keepers of God's laws. However, Jesus did not come as the keeper of God's laws nor as the witness of God's laws. He came as a witness of blessing. As a result, Jesus could not follow or be a part of Aaron's order. If Jesus had become the High Priest following Aaron's order, Jesus would also have been under the Law and would only have been a keeper and witness of God's laws. He would not have been able to bring salvation to mankind above the Law.

Jesus Christ came into the world to fulfill the Law that ruled the period of the Old Testament. He made a New Covenant for the era of the New Testament. He didn't come from the order of Aaron, but rather, He came from the order of Melchizedek.

Hebrews 7:1–3 says:

This Melchizedek was king of Salem and priest of God Most High. He met Abraham returning from the defeat of the kings and blessed him, and Abraham gave him a tenth of everything he possessed. First, his name means "king of righteousness"; then also, "king of Salem" means "king of peace." Without father or mother, without genealogy, without beginning of days or end of life, like the Son of God he remains a priest forever.

Melchizedek was without lineage and high birth, but he received a blessing from Abraham, the father of the Levites, to become a priest of God. In a similar way, Jesus was not of the Levite lineage, but He became the High Priest far surpassing any other priests, not only for the Israelites, but also for the whole world.

Having come as the High Priest for the world, the history of the world passed from the era of the Old Testament to the New. If anyone with faith should come before Jesus Christ, who became the High Priest for the world, he may also come before God.

ETERNAL SALVATION

For the high priest to be able to worship God and pray for the sins of the people, he must first understand the people. Only then can he ask for forgiveness from God with compassion and love. Jesus came to this world and suffered all the weaknesses of mankind. "For we do not have a high priest who is unable to sympathize with our weaknesses, but we have one who has been tempted in every way, just as we are—yet was without sin" (Heb. 4:15). Because Jesus came to the world in a physical body and suffered all its shortcomings, He understands our weaknesses. Furthermore, He obeyed God's will to the fullest and carried the cross.

When we are faced with a situation that seems like a life-threatening catastrophe, we must not despair and weep. The more we are faced with such calamities, the more we must come before Jesus to be strengthened. Jesus has experienced all our physical shortcomings.

He will answer our prayers. Not only that, but if we come before Jesus Christ, He will forgive all our sins and give us everlasting life. All believers have a High Priest—Jesus Christ. Jesus Christ shed His blood so that He could wash our sins with His blood.

Even while He walked on earth Jesus demonstrated His authority to cleanse—as is seen in His cleansing of the temple.

JESUS CHRIST WHO CLEANSED THE TEMPLE

With the coming of the Jewish holiday, Jesus went to the temple to worship. The temple was crowded with many vendors and buyers. The noise of the moneychangers, the cries of the animals and the various sounds of many people moving about were deafening.

Upon seeing such a sight, Jesus chased away the vendors and overturned the tables of the moneychangers. He exclaimed, "It is written . . . 'My house will be called a house of prayer,' but you are making it a 'den of robbers'" (Matt. 21:13).

Why did Jesus come to the temple to cleanse it of the moneychangers and vendors? What meaning does it have for us today?

THE MEANING OF THE RESTORATION OF THE TEMPLE

People came to the temple to worship God. However, at the time Jesus began His work, rather than being a place of worship, the temple had become a place where sacrificial animals were bought and sold and money was exchanged. It had become a place of business instead of a place to worship God.

The worshipers who came to the temple from distant areas had much trouble preparing the sacrifices for the worship. Most of them came near the temple and purchased the sacrificial animals or birds from the vendors. In addition, all males above the age of twenty were required to pay the fee of a half shekel as tax for the use of the temple. At the time, the money in circulation was the Roman coin. All people coming to the temple were required to change their Roman coins to Hebrew shekels.

Taking advantage of this situation, the vendors and the moneychangers made deals with the high priests. Fueled by the greed of the priests and the vendors, the worship of God became a mere formality and the temple became a place of business. Jesus raised His hand in anger and chased away the vendors and overturned the tables of the moneychangers and the sellers of doves.

JESUS WHO IS THE TEMPLE

Jesus Christ drove away the vendors and the moneychangers. "To those who sold doves he said, 'Get these out of here! How dare you turn my Father's house into a market!'" (John 2:16).

The Jews then crowded around Jesus Christ and asked, "What miraculous sign can you show us to prove your authority to do all this?" (v. 18). Jesus answered, "Destroy this temple, and I will raise it again in three days" (v. 19). The Jews then questioned Jesus, "This temple took forty-six years to build. How can you raise it in three days?"

When Jesus spoke of raising the temple, He was talking about the temple that was His body. The destruction of the temple and the raising of it referred to His dying on the cross and the resurrection that followed in three days.

THE REASON JESUS DESTROYED THE TEMPLE

Adam and Eve were created in the image of God; they enjoyed living in holiness in the Garden of Eden. They had the freedom to communicate with God. However, they succumbed to Satan's temptation and disobeyed God. After their disobedience, they fell from grace and were driven out of the Garden of Eden.

As a result, Adam's descendants lived in corruption and vileness. They lived in disobedience and disbelief. The ultimate destiny of such people was the judgment of God.

Jesus Christ came to this world to suffer on the cross, to have His physical body injured and to shed His blood in order to save us. He made it possible for us to live holy lives. Jesus destroyed the curse that leads men to a life of idolatry, trickery, jealousy and curse. In its place, Jesus established the order of life in love, hope, peace and holiness. He took responsibility of man's physical weakness by taking on the physical weakness of the human body Himself. After suffering death and being resurrected, Jesus Christ provided eternal life for His followers. Not only for our spirits, but for the life of righteousness while on earth, Jesus sent the blessed Holy Spirit to us on earth.

In this way, Jesus tore down and destroyed the temple that was His physical body and by doing so, He leads us to salvation and eternal life.

Anyone who comes into this new order that Jesus established for us shall live a life of holiness and no longer follow carnal desires. Those who have received the blessing of the blood must live as citizens of the kingdom of God and must communicate with God through the Holy Spirit.

OUR BODIES, THE TEMPLES OF GOD

The Bible tells us that our bodies are the temples of the Lord.

Don't you know that you yourselves are God's temple and that God's Spirit lives in you? If anyone destroys God's temple, God will destroy him; for God's temple is sacred, and you are that temple.
—1 CORINTHIANS 3:16–17

As God is holy, He cannot dwell in us when we are unholy. We must keep our bodies and minds holy with the help of the blood of Jesus Christ.

How can we keep our bodies holy when we ourselves are weak? We cannot become holy through any means of our own; however, through prayer, the Word of God and the help of the Holy Spirit, we can become holy (1 Tim. 4:5; 1 Pet. 1:2).

By acknowledging the Holy Spirit and receiving the Spirit, the Spirit will enter into our souls and fill us with holiness. Furthermore, we must pray in earnest, love God's Word and live according to the Word to keep our bodies holy as temples of God. Jesus Christ offered His own body on the cross so that we may become holy. The Holy Spirit uses our bodies as temples to lead us to live in holiness.

JESUS CHRIST AND THE EARLY CHURCH

Even after His ascension to heaven, Jesus has continued to work among His disciples and followers. After Christ's ascension, one hundred twenty followers were filled with the Holy Spirit. Although they could not see Jesus Christ with their own eyes, He was there in the form of the Holy Spirit.

After they were filled with the Holy Spirit they began spreading the gospel. Wherever they went they shouted, "Repent and be saved in the name of Jesus Christ." People repented and came to God. Although Jesus Christ is not with us physically, He comes to us as the Holy Spirit, and through the Holy Spirit He cures and heals us.

John and Peter, being filled with the Holy Spirit, performed many miracles. They saw a man sitting on the ground in front of the temple in Jerusalem. The man had been crippled since the day he was born. John and Peter healed the man's legs in the name of Jesus Christ, and the man began walking. Peter performed the miracle of bringing Dorcas back to life. After Paul met Jesus Christ in Damascus, he began to heal the sick by the power of God.

Jesus not only worked through His disciples, but He also worked through other Christians. Stephen, a deacon in the church, did great deeds that shine upon us today (Acts 6:8). When Philip was spreading the gospel in Samaria, many possessed by evil spirits were healed as well as cripples and paralytics (Acts 8:5–8). Jesus Christ still works with us today in the form of the Holy Spirit and does great works among us.

JESUS CHRIST OF TODAY

The greatest truth of Christianity is that Jesus does not live in some faraway and remote place, but He lives within us and continues to work among us. Jesus Christ makes His presence known through the Holy Spirit.

It is a great mistake for us to think that just because Christ ascended to heaven that He no longer concerns Himself with the world. Jesus Christ promised to make His presence known among Christians through the Holy Spirit. "I tell you the truth, anyone who has faith in me will do what I have been doing. He will do even greater things than these, because I am going to the Father" (John 14:12).

Years ago, I led a revival meeting in Chicago. In the congregation there was a woman suffering from a lump in her uterus. During the service, the woman approached me and said, "Reverend, I do not have any children. And I have a lump growing in my uterus. Doctors have informed me that they can remove the lump through surgery, but then I would not be able to have any children. I have no alternative but to turn to God for a miracle. Would you pray for me?" I prayed for her in Christ's name. Many years later, I received a letter from the woman. According to her letter, after our prayer, the lump disappeared completely, and she was blessed with healthy children. Jesus Christ works His miracles through those who believe in Him.

THE MANIFESTATION OF GOD'S POWER

For God's power to be manifested in our lives, the most important thing is to have faith. Jesus said:

I tell you the truth, if you have faith as small as a mustard seed, you can say to this mountain, "Move from here to there" and it will move. Nothing will be impossible for you.
—MATTHEW 17:20

We must believe that God's power and miracles will be manifested in our lives. And in order to have this faith, we must obey God's commands and stand firmly on His Word. To utilize God's powers and miracles, we must acknowledge the Holy Spirit, and as we welcome, accept and trust Him, we must pray with the help of the Holy Spirit. The Christ who is unchanging from the past to present still works His great miracles among us today. When we live in harmony with the Holy Spirit, we can experience Christ's miracles.

O living God, help us to come before You and open our hearts as we kneel before You and Jesus Christ, the High Priest for us all, so that we may receive the blessings You have for us. Bless us so that we may be led by the Holy Spirit to live to glorify You. As we pray while standing firmly on faith and Your Word, help us to experience the power of Jesus and the miracles of Jesus in our daily lives. In Christ's name, amen.

EIGHT

The Ministry of the Son

As children watch and listen to their parents, they begin to take on their character. As a result, parents with great character raise children with similar character. Parents who lack respect of others and are impatient in their character will raise children who have no regard for their elders and who are rough in their ways. The first role models for the children are the parents.

For those of us who believe in God and are born again, who is the role model for us? That role model is Jesus Christ and the Bible. We must learn through the Bible the great works of Jesus. As believers in Jesus Christ, much like the way children follow in the footsteps of their parents, we must take on the character of Jesus Christ.

THE MINISTRY OF SPREADING THE GOSPEL

Before starting His ministry in the world, following God's will, Jesus was baptized by John the Baptist in the Jordan River. Then, led by the Holy Spirit, Jesus went to the desert to be tempted by Satan. All of Satan's temptations were overcome with the Word of God. Afterward, Jesus spread the gospel of the kingdom of God and urged, "Repent, for the kingdom of heaven is near" (Matt. 4:17).

Jesus not only spread the gospel Himself, but He also commissioned His disciples to spread the Good News. He sent His twelve disciples into the known world and said to them:

As you go, preach this message: "The kingdom of heaven is near." Heal the sick, raise the dead, cleanse those who have leprosy, drive out demons. Freely you have received, freely give.
—MATTHEW 10:7–8

In addition, Jesus commanded the seventy followers to spread the gospel, "Heal the sick who are there and tell them, 'The kingdom of God is near you'" (Luke 10:9). He left the command for all His followers to spread the gospel and evangelize the world before His Second Coming.

All people and churches that wish to follow in Christ's footsteps must spread the gospel to the world. This is the true obedience of Christ's command.

THE MINISTRY OF TEACHING

Jesus was a teacher, and He taught the people about the gospel of heaven. Jesus left us many teachings, and He taught us how to pray. He taught on the beach, on Peter's boat and in various townships and countrysides. On the Sabbath, He taught at the temple and in synagogues.

When He taught the people about heaven, He used a variety of methods. Among the methods used by Jesus Christ, the most outstanding was the use of the parables. The parables of sowing seeds, the yeast, the prodigal son, the ten virgins and others showed examples of the kingdom of heaven.

Before His ascension to heaven, Jesus said:

Therefore go and make disciples of all nations,
baptizing them in the name of the Father and
of the Son and of the Holy Spirit, and teaching
them to obey everything I have commanded
you. And surely I am with you always, to the
very end of the age.
—MATTHEW 28:19–20

By saying this, He left His final command for us to spread the gospel throughout the earth.

For those of us who want to follow Christ's life, we must learn everything Christ taught us, and we must make sure His message is spread throughout the world.

THE MINISTRY OF HEALING THE SICK

Having come to provide salvation to the world, Christ spent two-thirds of His time healing the sick. Wherever He went, He healed the sick, and wherever He went, He was surrounded by the sick.

We get a glimpse of His healing by looking at Matthew 4:23–24:

Jesus went throughout Galilee, teaching in
their synagogues, preaching the good news of
the kingdom, and healing every disease and
sickness among the people. News about him
spread all over Syria, and people brought to
him all who were ill with various diseases,
those suffering severe pain, the demon-
possessed, those having seizures, and the
paralyzed, and he healed them.

Jesus went throughout the land and healed those who were suffering. Furthermore, He raised the dead. Jesus commanded the daughter of Jairus to rise from the dead (Luke 8:49–56); He brought forth from the coffin the only son of a widow in

Nain (Luke 7:11–15). And he raised Lazarus from death.

> Now a man named Lazarus was sick. He was
> from Bethany, the village of Mary and her
> sister Martha. This Mary, whose brother
> Lazarus now lay sick, was the same one who
> poured perfume on the Lord and wiped his
> feet with her hair. So the sisters sent word to
> Jesus, "Lord, the one you love is sick." When
> he heard this, Jesus said, "This sickness will
> not end in death. No, it is for God's glory so
> that God's Son may be glorified through it."
> —JOHN 11:1–4

Jesus said that anyone who believes in Him can receive the power to heal (Mark 16:17–18). After the ascension of Jesus Christ to heaven, His disciples received this power, and many of the sick were healed by their hands. The work of healing the sick is still done today as God has given this power to those with faith. We, as followers of Jesus Christ, must also receive this power to heal the sick.

Jesus Christ is the Great Shepherd who watches and protects our spirits, the Great Teacher who teaches us the truth about the kingdom of heaven and the Great Healer who heals all of our physical illnesses. These three roles were the roles of Jesus Christ, and they are also the roles for which we must strive. As disciples of Jesus Christ today, we must take upon ourselves the work of spreading the gospel and healing the sick.

It is as we understand the servanthood of Christ that we are motivated to complete the work of Jesus on earth. Jesus' ministry on earth was all about servanthood.

JESUS CHRIST THE SERVER

The climate of Palestine is very dry, and there is much sand that blows across the land. When people returned home from their travels, they had to wash the dirt and sand from their feet. When they invited a guest to supper, the master of the house made the servants wash the feet of the guests before dinner. This was a daily tradition.

Prior to His arrest by the Roman soldiers, Jesus and His disciples gathered together to celebrate the Passover. No one made a voluntary offer to wash the feet of Jesus Christ before supper.

The reason no one offered to do so was that in Judean society, the lowest person of the social hierarchy washed the feet of others. Because of this, each disciple looked to the other to do the task. Jesus Christ noticed this awkward situation, stood up, took off His robe, hung a towel around His waist and, with a wash basin, washed the feet of the disciples.

It was quite unprecedented to have one's teacher wash the feet of the followers. What Christ did was to teach the disciples a lesson, a lesson for us today.

THE LESSON FROM THE SILENCE

Christ's washing the feet of the disciples was a silent lesson and a shocking one since each disciple had been trying to raise himself above the other. Although the disciples had followed Jesus for three years and learned a great deal of His teachings, they did not understand the reason for which Jesus came to the world. To teach these disciples true wisdom, Jesus Christ shared the bread and wine with the disciples and told them of His coming death on the cross. As part of the night's lesson, Jesus washed the feet of each disciple. He became a model for the disciples to follow.

And whoever wants to be first must be slave of all. For even the Son of Man did not come to be served, but to serve, and to give his life as a ransom for many.
–MARK 10:44–45

Jesus also said, "I tell you the truth, no servant is greater than his master, nor is a messenger greater than the one who sent him. Now that you know these things, you will be blessed if you do them" (John 13:16–17). We must learn from the example of Jesus Christ and live to honor and serve others.

The word *service* in English contains a double meaning. One is applicable to the word *worship,* and the other is "doing something for the others," a self-sacrifice. For Christians the dual idea of worship and self-sacrifice cannot be separated. We must honor God in earnest by worshiping Him, and we must serve others with the love of Jesus Christ. When we honor our neighbors with the same attitude as we honor God, we will bear fruit and become the salt and light of the world.

THE COMPLETE SERVICE

Jesus prayed in the Garden of Gethsemane, "My Father, if it is possible, may this cup be taken from me" (Matt. 26:39). Through this prayer, we begin to fathom how great a suffering Christ faced bearing our sins.

But the final part of that prayer of Jesus Christ was, "Yet not as I will, but as you will." This was a manifestation of Christ's complete devotion and honor to God. Jesus was ready to take this great responsibility because He accepted that the suffering on the cross was according to God's will and would be a service done in self-sacrifice, not only to God, but also to mankind.

Who, being in the very nature God, did not consider equality with God something to be grasped, but made himself nothing, taking the very nature of a servant, being made in human likeness. And being found in appearance as a man, he humbled himself and became obedient to death—even death on a cross!
—PHILIPPIANS 2:6–8

Although Jesus Christ was God, He came to this world with a physical body. He was nailed to a cross to show His complete service to God. In response, God raised Jesus Christ from the grave. The Bible says, "Therefore God exalted him to the highest place and gave him the name that is above every name, that at the name of Jesus every knee should bow, in heaven and on earth and under the earth, and every tongue confess that Jesus Christ is Lord, to the glory of God the Father" (Phil. 2:9–11). We must not only accept the life of Jesus Christ who served God completely, but we must receive and reflect this image that is from Jesus Christ. By doing so, we become disciples and servants of the Lord.

Just as Jesus Christ served God and the disciples at the last supper, when we serve God and our neighbors, we can overcome hardships and adverse situations. Actually, hardships can make our faith grow, and they become conduits through which blessings can flow. No matter how long or how dark the tunnel of hardship may be, if we continue with the attitude of serving Jesus as well as our spouses and neighbors, we can overcome the hardship and turn it into a joyous victory.

As Christians, we must always live in service to others. We must not only serve Jesus Christ as our Savior, but we must also serve our parents, our spouses and our neighbors. When our enemies are hungry, we must feed them. By doing this, God will reward us in front of our enemies and fill our cups to overflowing.

Dear God, Help us all to become like Jesus in serving others as mature Christians and to glorify Your name. Help us to obey the command Jesus gave to us all to spread the gospel, teach Your words and heal the sick, so that You may be glorified and Your kingdom filled with Your worshipers. In the name of Jesus Christ, amen.

NINE

The Sacrifice of the Son

After Jesus Christ finished His prayer in the Garden of Gethsemane, He was arrested and taken to Caiaphas, the high priest. People spat on Christ's face, beat Him with fists, slapped Him with their hands, ridiculed Him and said, "Prophesy! Who hit you?" (Luke 22:64).

After the beating, Jesus Christ was taken to Pontius Pilate and was interrogated and whipped by the Roman soldiers. With every strike of the whip on Jesus' back, the flesh on His body was torn, and blood flowed from the wounds. They undressed Jesus Christ, clothed Him in a scarlet robe and put a crown of thorns on His head. The Roman soldiers struck Christ's head with a stick, spat at Him and said, "Hail, king of the Jews!" (Matt. 27:29). After having their fun, they dressed Him again in His clothes, dragged Him to the hill of Calvary and nailed Him on the cross.

At about three o'clock in the afternoon, Jesus could no longer bear His suffering in silence. He cried out, "My God, my God, why have you forsaken me?" (Matt. 27:46). He then shouted, "It is finished," and finally, "Father, into your hands I commit my spirit" (Luke 23:46). After His last words, He passed away.

Why did the Son of God, Jesus Christ, who was without any sin, suffer so much pain and suffering?

RELEASED FROM SADNESS AND SORROW

Sadness and sorrow are a binding to which all men have been shackled. Being under such a shackle, mankind could not have peace and had to struggle in despair. Jesus died on the cross to release man from his struggle against despair. If anyone should believe in Jesus Christ and depend on Him, he shall be released from sorrow and sadness.

Jesus calls out to those who suffer and lament from sadness and sorrow, "Come to me, all you who are weary and burdened, and I will give you rest" (Matt. 11:28). Those who believe in and depend on Jesus Christ shall be released from sadness and sorrow to receive the blessing of living in happiness.

RELEASE FROM FAULT AND SIN

When Jesus Christ was on the cross, both His hands and His feet were nailed to the cross with large nails. He had to wear a crown of thorns. His whole body was covered with wounds.

Why did the Son of God have to bear such harsh punishment? The reason Jesus suffered is because of our faults and sins. Every man has faults, both large and small. Man is also bound by sin, and he suffers because of sin. To release man from these two conditions, Jesus Christ had to suffer. The extent of His suffering can be understood by looking at Isaiah 52:14: "Just as there were many who were appalled at him—his appearance was so disfigured beyond that of any man and his form marred beyond human likeness."

By becoming the living sacrifice for our sins, Jesus Christ opened the door that leads to forgiveness, salvation and everlasting life. If any man will come to Christ and repent of his sins, his faults and sins will be forgiven, and he shall live in God's grace.

TO GIVE US PEACE

Because Adam and Eve disobeyed God and fell from His grace, God drove them away from the Garden of Eden. As a result, man has lived under the curse and despair. However, Jesus took the place of all men and wore the crown of thorns, which represented the curse. He was punished on the cross. Through this act, the relationship between God and mankind was restored, and man was given the right to live in peace with God. "Christ redeemed us from the curse of the law by becoming a curse for us, for it is written: 'Cursed is everyone who is hung on a tree'" (Gal. 3:13). There is nothing more precious than the grace and blessing afforded us by Jesus Christ. The blessing that is Jesus Christ is the only gift with any value that we may receive when we repent to God.

TO CURE THE SICK

Every time Jesus Christ received lashes by the Roman soldiers, His flesh was torn, and He suffered as His body was injured. The lashes that Jesus Christ suffered represented the suffering of sin and disease from which man could not escape.

God wants to cure us from disease and illness. God wants us to be blessed with the blood of Jesus Christ so that we might be cured of sickness of the spirit, sickness of the body and sickness of our souls so that we may live in complete health. Jesus Christ extends His nail-scarred hands, calling out to the people who are suffering from sickness and disease. The prophet Isaiah said, "We all, like sheep, have gone astray, each of us has turned to his own way; and the LORD has laid on Him the iniquity of us all" (Isa. 53:6).

Many people ignore the blessing that is Jesus Christ, and they follow a path of their own making. They are anxious to gain fame, authority and wealth. They seek to find a comfortable life for their physical bodies. Their pursuits ignore the blessing of Christ's death on the cross. In reference to these people, the psalmist said, "A man who has riches without understanding is like the beasts that perish" (Ps. 49:20). Only those who answer the invitation of Jesus Christ can be reconciled to God and experience God's grace.

Even today, Jesus speaks and calls to us to open our hearts and come before Him. We must realize the meaning of the suffering that Jesus bore and answer His calling. Then, God will fill us with His blessings.

THE CROSS THAT JESUS CHRIST BORE IN OUR PLACE

Barabbas committed a heinous crime and was sentenced to die. He had nothing more to do in life but to wait for the day of his execution. Finally, he had one day left before his execution. His last night must have been long, and he must have been in despair.

With the rising sun, he was pulled from jail. In fear of his impending death and the lack of sleep, Barabbas must have been tense as he stared out with his bloodshot eyes. He must have felt like a wild animal being taken to slaughter. But unbelievable news was delivered to his ears. A guard came to Barabbas and said, "You are free. Go wherever you want to go. Jesus will bear the cross in your place."

Barabbas gathered his wits, and with indescribable happiness, he started off in a direction away from death. At the same time, Jesus Christ was carrying the cross, being whipped by soldiers, stumbling and falling from His struggle and slowly making His way up to Calvary. Before we received the blessing of salvation, all of us were like the criminal Barabbas. But because Jesus bore the cross in our place, we have been freed from death.

THE MEANING OF THE CROSS

Christ does not want us to suffer from sicknesses of the spirit, the heart and the body. Instead, Jesus came in order to give us new life and to protect us from the demons that steal, kill and destroy. Jesus wants to give us overflowing blessings. In order to do this, He took all our sickness upon Himself and died on the cross. "He himself bore our sins in his body on the tree, so that we might die to sins and live for righteousness; by his wounds you have been healed" (1 Pet. 2:24).

Whenever we look at the cross, we must think about its meaning. The cross on which Jesus died is the cross that can free us from despair and sadness.

Jesus was nailed on the cross because God willed it. Although we deserved death and the curse because of our sinfulness and vileness, Jesus Christ died to save us from eternal death. His death washed away the sins of not only the people of Israel, but also the sins of all men.

Our sins have been eternally cleansed by the grace of the cross. No matter how we may try, we cannot become righteous through our own work. We can only become righteous when our sins are forgiven through faith in Jesus Christ.

Those who deny that Jesus died on the cross for our sins and do not believe in the healing power of the blood cannot escape God's judgment. Jesus said, "I told you that you would die in your sins; if you do not believe that I am the one I claim to be, you will indeed die in your sins" (John 8:24). Only through faith and accepting that Jesus Christ bore the cross for our sins can we receive eternal life and escape the eternal curse and death.

Jesus Christ was forsaken by God, and He was hung high on the cross between heaven and earth. As He hung on the cross, He cried, "My God, my God, why have you forsaken me?" (Matt. 27:46). Why was Jesus Christ rejected and forsaken by God? Jesus was rejected and forsaken by God because of our sin. He bore our sins. When He became sin for us, God could not look upon Him.

After Adam and Eve had committed their first sin, mankind was tainted with sin and could not reach the glory of God (Rom. 3:23). Man was in the position of being an enemy of God. Jesus died on the cross in our place, and we have been reconciled to God and allowed to be a part of the glory that is His.

If we come before God through Jesus Christ, God adopts us as His children. If we are chosen to be God's children, we shall be freed from despair and be led to the land of milk and honey. Jesus Christ died on the cross in our place so that we may receive eternal life.

SEVEN STATEMENTS FROM THE CROSS

After Jesus finished praying in the Garden of Gethsemane, He was arrested. Afterward, He was hung on the cross. Jesus Christ, wearing the crown of thorns, both hands and feet nailed and bleeding profusely from the injuries inflicted by the Roman soldiers, suffered on the cross from nine o'clock in the morning to three o'clock in the afternoon. As He suffered, He made seven statements. His statements teach us some important lessons. They also serve as an important guide for confirming the meaning of salvation and the role that Christians must assume.

1. "FORGIVE THEM."

When our eyes are closed, we cannot see what is in front of us. Similarly, the descendants of Adam and Eve, whose spiritual eyes were blinded, could not see the Messiah who came to save the world. Instead, they committed the crime of nailing Him to the cross. Having committed this grave crime, they could not even recognize the gravity of their crime and the judgment that would surely follow. But Jesus saw them with pity and prayed for them, "Father, forgive them" (Luke 23:34).

Jesus Christ wants to forgive all people with measureless compassion and mercy. Whosoever comes to Jesus Christ, repents of his sins and accepts Him as Savior shall be forgiven and shall lead a new life.

2. "YOU SHALL BE WITH ME IN HEAVEN."

On either side of Jesus Christ on Calvary were two robbers. Feeling the incredible pain on the cross, one of the robbers cried, "Aren't you the Christ? Save yourself and us!" (Luke 23:39).

The second robber pleaded to Jesus, "Jesus, remember me when you come into your kingdom." Jesus answered the second robber, "I tell you the truth, today you will be with me in paradise" (vv. 42–43).

The two robbers were heinous criminals. But Jesus did not ask what the robbers' crimes were, but instead, no matter what were their crimes, the robber who repented Jesus accepted as a child of God.

When a person accepts Jesus Christ as Savior, he sheds the dead physical flesh of the cursed man and is made anew to live eternally with Jesus Christ where there are no tears, worries, sorrows or deaths.

3. "DEAR WOMAN . . . "

When Jesus was nailed on the cross, His parents, His aunt, Caiaphas' wife and Mary Magdalene were at Calvary. Even in the great pain and suffering on the cross, Jesus Christ was concerned about His mother. As He looked at John, He said, "Dear woman, here is your son" (John 19:26). Then He said to His disciple, "Here is your mother." John took care of Mary in his house (v. 27).

Through this we can see that Jesus Christ honored His physical parents. The Bible emphasizes, "If anyone does not provide for his relatives, and especially for his immediate family, he has denied the faith and is worse than an unbeliever" (1 Tim. 5:8). Even as Jesus was dying, He did not forget His filial piety. We must emulate Christ's love and respect our parents.

4. "ELOI, ELOI, LAMA SABACHTHANI?"

While Jesus was on earth, He was in constant communication and fellowship with God. Then as Christ went up Calvary, God forsook Jesus; their fellowship was severed for the first time. Why was Jesus Christ forsaken by God? The reason was because Jesus Christ bore the sins of all mankind.

"Eloi, Eloi, lama sabachthani?", or "My God, my God, why have you forsaken me?" (Matt. 27:46; Mark 15:34) is a cry of sorrow that Jesus Christ spoke as He was overcome by suffering on the cross. To the extent of being forsaken by God, Jesus Christ had to suffer taking the place of mankind. Jesus Christ paid a great price to offer us salvation.

5. "I AM THIRSTY."

Jesus Christ shed His blood upon the cross and suffered a very natural human craving. He thirsted. As He was dying on the cross, He must have felt the thirst not only physically, but also spiritually and emotionally. Jesus said, "I am thirsty" (John 19:28).

The reason Jesus Christ suffered thirst on the cross was so that He could quench our spiritual and physical thirst. Christ suffered this extreme pain of thirst and has allowed the spring of life to flow out of all Christians (John 7:38).

6. "It is finished."

His statement "It is finished" represents a great victory (John 19:30). Jesus completely paid the debt for sin, death, the curse and despair. Jesus Christ, who is God, wore the physical body of a man. He came into the world and died on the cross. He has cleared all our debts. His death has freed man from evil and eternal death and has given man the right to live in freedom.

7. "Into your hand I commit my spirit."

Before Jesus passed away, He showed us where our spirits can find rest. "Father, into your hands I commit my spirit" (Luke 23:46). He shows us that our spirits should belong to God. With our spirits in God, we must worship God with all our hearts, bodies and spirits.

Through these seven statements spoken by Jesus upon the cross, we learn of the love Jesus has for mankind. Jesus is both God and man. Jesus Christ who came to this world to save the human race lived a life of absolute obedience to God, absolute worship of God and absolute faith in God. Because of what Jesus did, God was glorified. God invites all of us to kneel before Jesus Christ and worship Him.

Our salvation did not become possible through an accident. Our salvation is a result of Jesus Christ suffering the worst possible pain and tragedy. Through the cross mankind was given the possibility of being saved.

TWO KINDS OF CROSS

The Bible speaks of two kinds of crosses. One is the cross that Jesus Christ carried in our place; the second is the cross that we must bear ourselves. Many Christians are in a state of confusion regarding these two crosses. Some people think that they should bear both of the crosses, and being burdened by their weight, they suffer needlessly. Others think neither of the crosses were meant for them but for Christ, and their spiritual lives and faith are stagnant. For us to become mature Christians, we must correctly recognize and understand the meaning of the two crosses.

THE CROSS OF JESUS CHRIST

Jesus Christ came into this world to free us from Satan's clutches by bearing the cross. There is no need for us to bear that cross because Jesus has already suffered on that cross. From what did Jesus Christ redeem us on that cross?

First, Jesus Christ redeemed us from our sins. He took upon Himself all the past, present and future sins of the world. His body was crucified in order to clear us of our sins, and because of what Jesus did, there is no reason for us to be tormented by the weight of our sins.

Second, Jesus Christ redeemed us from sickness and disease. He suffered physically in order to free us from our own physical sufferings. Jesus spent much of His time during His ministry healing the sick. It is clear evidence that sickness and disease were not meant for mankind.

Third, Jesus Christ redeemed us from the curse. Some people who live in extreme poverty console themselves by saying, "This is my cross to bear." However, other than poverty required by some special calling from God, poverty should not be a cross that a person should bear.

God wants us to live in abundance so that we may and help our neighbors (2 Cor. 9:8, 11). Pains of sin, disease, poverty and failure are not crosses that we should have to bear. All of these were already carried by Christ. When such hardships approach us, we must drive them away in Christ's name and live in peace, forgiveness and blessing.

OUR CROSS

Jesus said, "Anyone who does not take his cross and follow me is not worthy of me" (Matt. 10:38). What does the personal cross that Jesus mentioned imply?

First, the personal cross refers to the life that overcomes the desire of the self. In Galatians 5:24, Paul says, "Those who belong to Christ Jesus have crucified the sinful nature with its passions and desires." We must deny ourselves the desires of the flesh, the desires of the mind and the pride of this world. Instead, we must take upon ourselves the cross by making an effort to live like Jesus Christ.

Second, the personal cross refers to the suffering we incur in order to follow Jesus Christ. Paul was born to a good family and given a good education. Having the skill as a tent maker, he could have lived a simple and easy life of faith. Despite all of his good fortune, he chose the difficult path of becoming a witness of the gospel. This was a cross that Paul decided to carry in order to follow Christ's command.

Third, a personal cross refers to the persecution that a person receives because of his belief in Jesus Christ. This is perhaps the greatest cross for anyone to bear. When people believe in Jesus, they suffer persecution from home and family for their faith in Jesus Christ. But in the end, many cases where a Christian overcomes persecution from their families may lead their families to salvation. This kind of persecution should be embraced by all Christians in order to glorify God.

Living according to God's will, spreading the gospel and being persecuted for faith in God are all personal crosses that we should bear gladly. We should not refuse or avoid these personal crosses, and we should pray in earnest to receive strength to overcome persecutions.

THE BLESSINGS OF THE CROSS

When we carry our personal crosses and come before God, we will receive great blessings. As we overcome ourselves and endure the burdens of our personal crosses, God will find pleasure in us. Those who deny their crosses and love the world, no matter how much they may cry out in prayer, God will not answer them. But if a person denies himself and follows after Jesus Christ while carrying his cross, God hears that person's prayers and gladly answers. When we carry the cross, we will be filled with happiness. Paul said, "We always carry around in our body the death of Jesus, so that the life of Jesus may also be revealed in our body" (2 Cor. 4:10). When we manage to carry our personal crosses, the resurrection of Jesus Christ will be present in our hearts.

When we faithfully carry our crosses, our rewards are being prepared in heaven. Jesus said, "Blessed are you when people insult you, persecute you and falsely say all kinds of evil against you because of me. Rejoice and be glad, because great is your reward in heaven, for in the same way they persecuted the prophets who were before you" (Matt. 5:11–12). If we faithfully carry the cross and endure the persecution resulting from our faith, when Jesus comes to the world the second time God will reward us and put on our heads the crowns of glory.

There are crosses that we must carry. There are also crosses that we need not carry. We must decide which ones we should carry and then carry them gladly. When we do so, the glory of God will fill us.

O living God, help us to fully understand the meaning of the pain You suffered on the cross, and help us to be guided by this understanding. Make us into true Christians who can share in the pain and give our lives in sacrifice for Your glory. Help us to deny ourselves and carry our crosses, and as we follow in the footsteps of Jesus Christ, help us to live lives worthy of His disciples. In Christ's name, amen.

TEN

The Victory of the Son

After a cold winter, spring comes. The earth begins to stir and find life once again. Water flows through branches that looked as if they were dead. The hills become alive with flowers, and the songs of the birds fill the air.

Similarly, for those of us who were made in God's image, our lives do not end with the death of our physical bodies. Jesus Christ died on the cross to redeem us from our sins, and through His resurrection, He has given us eternal life.

If Jesus Christ had not redeemed us on the cross and through His resurrection, we would wander through life in sin and be eternally cursed and die. However, through the redemption on the cross and the resurrection from death, whenever anyone accepts Jesus Christ, his body will also die and be made anew.

THE PROOF OF CHRIST'S RESURRECTION

As Jesus died on the cross, the priests and the Pharisees

113

remembered what Jesus had said about being resurrected from the dead in three days. So, they blocked the entrance to His tomb with a great rock and had the Roman soldiers guard the grave to prevent anyone from getting into the tomb. Then, on the third day, Jesus overcame death and was resurrected.

After the Sabbath, at dawn on the first day of the week, Mary Magdalene and the other Mary went to look at the tomb. There was a violent earthquake, for an angel of the Lord came down from heaven and, going to the tomb, rolled back the stone and sat on it. His appearance was like lightning, and his clothes were white as snow. The guards were so afraid of him that they shook and became like dead men.
–MATTHEW 28:1–4

Upon hearing the news of Christ's resurrection, the priests were overcome with fear. They paid the Roman soldiers to spread the false rumor that His disciples had stolen His body. Prior to Christ's capture by the Roman soldiers, He was abandoned by all of His disciples, who fled in fear. How could such timid disciples have enough courage to fight with the Roman soldiers guarding the tomb and steal the body?

After the resurrection of Christ, the disciples risked their lives to witness to the resurrection of Christ. All the disciples, except John, were martyred. If the resurrection of Jesus Christ was a fabrication by the disciples, why would the disciples have risked and even given up their lives for such a lie? There is nothing more foolish than sacrificing one's life to be a witness to something that is false.

We can be assured of the resurrection of Jesus Christ through the presence of the Holy Spirit. When Jesus was arrested, Peter betrayed Jesus Christ on three separate occasions. But after having received the Holy Spirit, he was able to become a confident witness of the resurrection: "God has raised this Jesus to life, and we are all witnesses of the fact. Exalted to the right hand of God, he has received from the Father the promised Holy Spirit and has poured out what you now see and hear" (Acts 2:32–33).

If the Holy Spirit resides among us, the fact of Christ's resurrection and the fact that Jesus does His work among us even today become certain. In addition, the church, which the Holy Spirit has established, is the fruit of Christ's resurrection.

In the past two thousand years the church, which represents the body of Jesus Christ, has been established in countless numbers, and the fact that through the innumerable churches, the gospel has been spread throughout the world attests to the resurrection of Jesus Christ.

THE RESULT OF CHRIST'S RESURRECTION

In the museums of Cairo, Egypt there are many mummies of the pharaohs who ruled Egypt three thousand years ago. Although the golden coffins of those pharaohs are still magnificent and unchanged, the pharaohs themselves are now nothing more than mere dried bones.

While the remains of all the saints and great men are still in their graves, the grave of Jesus Christ is empty. Jesus Christ is not in some grave waiting for the worshipers to visit Him, but rather He arose from His grave and meets us through the Holy Spirit.

For what I received I passed on to you as of first importance: that Christ died for our sins according to the Scriptures, that he was buried, that he was raised on the third day according to the Scriptures.

—1 Corinthians 15:3–4

For those Judeans who wanted a sign, Jesus Christ prophesied about His resurrection by telling them about the three days Jonah stayed in the stomach of a great fish and the parable of demolishing and raising the temple in three days.

Jesus also said, "Do not be afraid. I am the First and the Last. I am the Living One; I was dead, and behold I am alive for ever and ever! And I hold the keys of death and Hades" (Rev. 1:17–18). Jesus Christ, the Son of God, not only paid for your sins on the cross, but He also conquered Hades, or hell. Because of Jesus Christ, Satan has been defeated and can no longer exercise his authority of death, sickness and condemnation over us. Whosoever believes in Jesus Christ and His resurrection shall be released from sin, condemnation and death to inherit the glory of the kingdom of heaven.

LIFE OF A WITNESS

For those who believe in the resurrection of Jesus Christ, their whole lives must change to become witnesses to Christ's resurrection. All followers must use the language appropriate for those with the belief in the resurrection. "It's not possible, I can't do that, I am a failure, I am a loser" are not the words of faith.

Jesus said, "I tell you the truth, whatever you bind on earth will be bound in heaven, and whatever you loose on earth will be loosed in heaven" (Matt. 18:18). Jesus Christ who was resurrected from the dead works His miracles today. We must always be positive in the Holy Spirit, aggressive in our goals, creative and positive in our daily speech. By living this way, we reflect the belief in the resurrection of Jesus Christ.

In addition, we must go out to the world and be witnesses to the resurrection of Jesus Christ, which has given all of us the hope for life. We must become strong witnesses to revive those who have become tired of life and those who are dejected. Those who believe in the resurrection of Jesus will not only experience the miracles of God, but they will also participate in the great resurrection in heaven. Because of Christ's victory over death and His resurrection, all Christians have received the promise of everlasting life. As witnesses of Christ's resurrection, we are called to spread this hope of everlasting life to those who do not believe.

THE EVIDENCE OF THE RESURRECTION

The Bible teaches that because Jesus Christ was resurrected in three days all Christians will also be resurrected at the moment of Christ's Second Coming. Such is the hope Jesus Christ gave to all those who believe in Him. His resurrection creates a new world, a new order of life. It affords mankind the ultimate answer. Where can we look for evidence that Jesus Christ was indeed resurrected?

CONFIRMED BY WITNESSES

After having received the Holy Spirit at the Day of Pentecost, Peter said, "God has raised this Jesus to life, and we are all witnesses of the fact. Exalted to the right hand of God, he has received from the Father the promised Holy Spirit and has poured out what you now see and hear" (Acts 2:32–33). He continued, "Repent and be baptized, every one of you, in the name of Jesus Christ for the forgiveness of your sins. And you will receive the gift of the Holy Spirit" (v. 38). Peter, who had denied Jesus three times before receiving the Holy Spirit, became a brave witness. If we accept the Holy Spirit as Peter did and say, "I am in the Lord and the Lord is in me," we shall also experience the confirmation of Christ's resurrection. By experiencing the Holy Spirit, we receive the assurance of Christ's resurrection.

DEMONSTRATED BY RESURRECTION POWER

Adam's fall from grace has caused mankind to become a "diseased being." Our spirits were corrupted, our hearts were filled with dread and anxiety and our bodies have suffered from all sorts of diseases. Simply put, our whole being has suffered from various afflictions. Not only personally, but families, societies, countries and the whole world lay on the sickbed with the disease of wars and inhumanity caused by man's sins. However, the power of Christ's resurrection can completely heal these diseases and provide new health and hope to the world.

One day, as Peter and John were going into a temple, a cripple who was sitting near the entrance saw them and pleaded with them. Upon seeing the beggar, Peter said, "Silver or gold I do not have, but what I have I give you. In the name of Jesus Christ of Nazareth, walk" (Acts 3:6) With those words, Peter lifted the cripple. The cripple began to feel strength coming to his legs. He stood up strong, jumped and ran, glorifying and praising God. The people saw what had happened, and they were amazed. Peter witnessed to them:

You disowned the Holy and Righteous One
and asked that a murderer be released to you.
You killed the author of life, but God raised
him from the dead. We are witnesses of this.
—ACTS 3:14–15

Peter was captured and taken to the Judean authorities for spreading the gospel. He said, "It is by the name of Jesus Christ of Nazareth, whom you crucified but whom God raised from the dead, that this man stands before you healed" (Acts 4:10) The healing of the sick is one proof of Christ's resurrection.

The name of the risen Christ has the power to treat our diseased spirits and restore our images to that of God's.

Christ's name also heals our hearts and frees us from fear and anxiety.

ESTABLISHED BY COMMUNITY

During the period of the early church, as the disciples witnessed about Christ's resurrection, many people were blessed by God; from their hearts flowed faith, hope and love. As a result, a movement of sharing began among the disciples. The followers of Christ shared their faith, hope and love, and they shared food and clothing as well as places to stay. The selfish attitude of "provide only for me" prevents a person from fully experiencing the miracle of Christ's resurrection. We must share with our family, our brothers and neighbors.

When we continuously practice the act of sharing, we not only experience the miracle of the resurrection, but we also become tools for witnessing the great resurrection of our living Christ.

THE NEW LIFE IN THE RESURRECTION

People often say, "Having faith in anything is beneficial in some ways. No matter what that faith may be in, it is not bad." However, for some reason, there are people who take an active dislike toward the resurrection of Jesus Christ.

In the period of the early church, such reaction to Christ and the Christian faith made it difficult for Christians. Many people were swayed by the Hellenistic philosophy that said the soul itself was indestructible; once the body died, it became a handful of dust.

People swayed by this philosophy could not accept the fact that Christ was resurrected physically and that Christians would also be resurrected physically when Christ returns. The conflict caused them to stir up difficulty and trouble for the Corinthian church. Is faith in the Christian resurrection a lie?

THE TRUTH
OF THE RESURRECTION

The seasonal changes of nature illustrate the law of the resurrection. When autumn comes, the leaves wither and fall from the trees. When the cold storms of winter blow, the trees look as if they are dead. But when the winter passes and spring returns, leaves begin to grow as water begins to rise up through the trees. By summer, trees are full of green leaves. When we observe this law of nature, we not only see the existence of the law of death, but we can understand the existence of the law of resurrection.

The law of resurrection does not end with plants and trees. Jesus said, "I am the resurrection and the life. He who believes in me will live, even though he dies; and whoever lives and believes in me will never die. Do you believe this?" (John 11:25–26).

Paul said, "But if it is preached that Christ has been raised from the dead, how can some of you say that there is no resurrection of the dead? If there is no resurrection of the dead, then not even Christ has been raised" (1 Cor. 15:12–13). Because Jesus was resurrected from the dead, we also will be resurrected after our deaths.

Furthermore, Paul teaches that we will not only be resurrected, but after our resurrection, we will also be in a different form from our earthly one: "It is sown in dishonor, it is raised in glory; it is sown in weakness, it is raised in power; it is sown a natural body, it is raised a spiritual body" (1 Cor. 15:43–44). We now have a body appropriate for living on this Earth. We shall have a body form for living in heaven (1 Cor. 15:49).

THE FIRST FRUIT OF RESURRECTION

Paul said:

Regarding his Son, who as to his human

nature was a descendant of David, and who
through the Spirit of holiness was declared
with power to be the Son of God by his resurrection from the dead: Jesus Christ our Lord.
—ROMANS 1:3–4

The reason mankind is bound by the law of death is
because of sin. Jesus Christ, who was the only begotten Son
of God, came to this world to save the human race. He died
on the cross and was resurrected from the dead in three days;
thereby He redeemed us from sin.

There are many evidences of the resurrection of Christ.
The disciples saw the resurrected Christ. Thomas even
touched the nail-scarred hand of Jesus. The disciples and five
hundred of His followers saw Jesus ascending to heaven. The
greatest witness is the Holy Spirit.

Luke says, "Exalted to the right hand of God, he has
received from the Father the promised Holy Spirit and has
poured out what you now see and hear" (Acts 2:33). The
Holy Spirit's work of coming into our hearts is the greatest
proof we have of Jesus Christ's resurrection.

THE NEW LIFE
OF THE RESURRECTION

Those who believe in Jesus Christ will receive the new life of
the resurrection. "For since death came through a man, the
resurrection of the dead comes also through a man. For as in
Adam all die, so in Christ all will be made alive" (1 Cor.
15:21–22). The old selves have died on the cross with Jesus
Christ. Just as Jesus Christ was resurrected, we, in unison
with Jesus Christ, will be resurrected and receive eternal life.

This new life shall be given to us by Jesus Christ, who proclaimed, "I am the resurrection and the life" (John 11:25).
And all those who have received the new life shall live
together with Jesus Christ in God's kingdom forever.

RESURRECTION AND HOPE

If man did not have hope for tomorrow, he would surely perish. After Jesus proclaimed, "Repent. The kingdom of God is at hand," He forgave sinners, healed the sick, drove away the evil spirits, raised the dead and gave hope to the people. People drowning in hopelessness came to Jesus Christ. The charisma of Jesus Christ, who proclaimed the secret of the kingdom of God with unnatural power, stirred all Israel.

The disciples of Christ swelled with pride that they had been chosen, and they were filled with hope of taking their places with Jesus Christ in the kingdom of God. They thought that Israel would soon be freed from Rome. As prophesied in the Bible, they expected the Messiah's kingdom to be established on earth. With such compassion, they followed diligently after Jesus Christ.

When Jesus warned them of His own coming death, the disciples were greatly shocked. Judas Iscariot was so disappointed and angered that he betrayed Jesus.

The disciples saw Jesus dying on the cross. Their dreams and hopes were shattered. On top of this, the Roman soldiers and the Judean authorities sought to capture and kill all of Christ's disciples. For the disciples the despair was indescribable.

HOPE IN THE MIDST OF DESPAIR

After Jesus' death the disciples entered into mourning. Their mourning continued to the next day and the day following. There were no changes. The Roman soldiers continued to stand guard at Christ's grave. The disciples thought, *Jesus has departed from this world forever.*

On the morning of the third day, the sorrow-filled mother

of Christ, along with other grieving women, came to the tomb to sprinkle perfume on the corpse. As they came to the grave, they worried about how they would move the great rock that blocked the entrance to the tomb.

Amazingly, the rock had already been rolled away. When they entered the tomb, they could not find the body of Christ. An angel said to them, "Why do you look for the living among the dead? He is not here; he has risen! Remember how he told you, while he was still with you in Galilee" (Luke 24:5–6).

In their joy and amazement, they ran to the house where Peter and John were staying and told them what they had seen. Upon hearing this news, Peter and John ran to the tomb. Peter went into the tomb and discovered that the body of Jesus Christ had vanished with nothing left except the funeral robe.

The resurrected Christ appeared to two disciples as they were on their way back to Emmaus. Jesus began to explain the prophetic passages in the Bible and helped the two disciples understand and realize that He had been resurrected.

Jesus confirmed His resurrection again by appearing before Thomas, who had said that he would not believe that Christ had risen until he himself had felt the nail-scarred hands and side. Jesus allowed Thomas to see Him. Jesus appeared to many disciples in the next forty days to allow them to witness the fact of His resurrection.

THE MEANING OF THE RESURRECTION TODAY

First, the resurrection of Christ clearly confirms that we have been freed from our sins forever. Jesus Christ took upon Himself all of our sins. With all of our sins upon Him, Jesus entered the "prison of death." Jesus did not enter the prison of death to redeem His own sins, but to redeem us from our sins.

If Jesus had entered death and was unable to pay for our sins, then He would not have become our Savior. However, Jesus carried the sins of all men, went into the prison of death, paid for all of our sins and came out of the prison in His resurrected body. As a result, if any man comes before Jesus Christ with all his sins, through the grace of Jesus Christ, all his sins will be forgiven, and he will be declared righteous.

Second, the resurrection of Christ proves that our lives shall never again be meaningless. We have come to learn that God is a living God, and the purpose of our lives is to glorify Him. The resurrection of Christ gives us a purpose in life. A person who lacks this knowledge lacks a purpose in life regardless of how many worldly possessions he may have. What good is it to have all the things of this world if you don't have life?

Our first priority in life should be to believe in Jesus Christ and to glorify the Lord. If our purpose is based on our fame and wealth, such successes will be meaningless after death. Only faith in the resurrection provides us with an eternal purpose and value for our lives.

Third, the resurrection of Christ verifies the eternal victory over death. Can a man live after his physical death? This has been a question asked by all men since the beginning of time. The answer to this question is provided only by Jesus Christ. Jesus has shown us by coming to this world as a man, dying on the cross to redeem us from sin and being resurrected from death that there is eternal life for those who believe. He said, "I am the resurrection and the life. He who believes in me will live, even though he dies; and whoever lives and believes in me will never die" (John 11:25–26). Because Jesus Christ conquered death, we can be assured of our eternal life in Christ.

Dear God of mercy, we thank You for the hope of the salvation You gave to us through Christ's victory over death. Help us to live victorious lives in this world as we grasp onto the promise of everlasting life. Let every Christian know that the seed of resurrection has been planted in their souls. In Christ's name, amen.

ELEVEN

The Legacy of the Son

Through the Bible we see that whenever God changed the destiny of a person, He also gave the person a new name. The reason for such practice was because the name of a person was important.

As Jesus finished His ministry and left this world, He left His name as legacy to the disciples. The legacy is also available to all Christians who believe in Jesus Christ today.

We see many Christians who do not depend on the name of Jesus Christ. They are unable to come before God confidently. Jesus said, "You may ask me for anything in my name, and I will do it" (John 14:14). In the name of Jesus Christ, we can pray to God confidently and have our prayers answered. But this does not mean that we can use the power of His name in any way we wish. We can use the name of Jesus Christ only when we live in obedience. Christ's name has great power, authority and strength, and God has granted Christians the right to use the name of Jesus Christ.

This name of Jesus Christ has great power and authority. The name of Jesus Christ represents the power and the authority of the One who created the universe. Receiving the name of Jesus Christ as legacy means that we have received the power and authority of Jesus Christ as lawful heirs, and we have received the heavenly blessing of divinity and the worldly blessing of fruitfulness.

The Bible says, "Salvation is found in no one else, for there is no other name under heaven given to men by which we must be saved" (Acts 4:12). The right to be forgiven and receive salvation is available only for those who believe and depend on Jesus Christ. Christians have been given a special authority to save many dying souls by spreading the name of Jesus Christ.

Jesus Christ was nailed to the cross and resurrected in three days so that He could give us the authority and power of His name. Anyone who calls out to Jesus will receive salvation.

Those of us who have received the legacy of the name and have become the rightful heirs of Christ's authority must take upon ourselves the work of spreading the gospel to family members, relatives and neighbors.

The great work of spreading the gospel has been given to all of us. For those who have received such legacy, we must obey Christ's command: "Go into all the world and preach the good news to all creation. Whoever believes and is baptized will be saved, but whoever does not believe will be condemned" (Mark 16:15–16). We must make every effort to spread the gospel.

LIVING BY FAITH

Rather than basing our faith on some formalized religious concepts, we must live in faith with the power of the Holy Spirit. The Holy Spirit comes to our hearts and destroys our evil desires. He helps us to pray. He helps us to understand the Bible. He helps us to fill our duties as members of the church. The help of the Holy Spirit is indispensable. Jesus said, "If you then, though you are evil, know how to give good gifts to your children, how much more will your Father in heaven give the Holy Spirit to those who ask him!" (Luke 11:13). God sent us the Holy Spirit as promised after Christ's ascension to heaven.

With faith in the name of Jesus Christ we must pray to be filled with the Holy Spirit, and we must greet, welcome and accept the Holy Spirit into our hearts. When we do so, the Holy Spirit enters our heart to strengthen our weaknesses and leads us to victory.

Those who believe in Jesus Christ and have received the name of Christ as legacy are the lawful representatives of Christ who have received the power to drive out demons and cure the sick. Jesus said:

And these signs will accompany those who believe: In my name they will drive out demons; they will speak in new tongues; they will pick up snakes with their hands; and when they drink deadly poison, it will not hurt them at all; they will place their hands on sick people, and they will get well.
—MARK 16:17–18

As witnessed by this verse, we have been given the authority to drive out demons in the name of Christ and to pray for those suffering from illnesses so that they can be blessed with healing.

Today, the world is filled with evil spirits, and many people are demoralized spiritually and killed physically by demons. The authority to drive out demons and heal others in the name of Christ can glorify God and act as a proof of the existence of the power of God.

EXPERIENCING THE LIFE OF JESUS CHRIST

Two thousand years ago, the people who were the contemporaries of Jesus Christ were able to see Jesus in person, hear His voice and observe His deeds. Afterward, Jesus Christ died on the cross, was resurrected and ascended into heaven. Today, Jesus sits at the right hand of God. For those of us who did not live two thousand years ago, how can we meet Jesus and experience His life? Let's examine the steps to experiencing the Christ-life.

BE FILLED WITH THE HOLY SPIRIT

After the Day of Pentecost, Peter, being filled with the Holy Spirit, said to the crowd, "God has raised this Jesus to life, and we are all witnesses of the fact" (Acts 2:32).

After Jesus ascended to heaven, He sent us the Holy Spirit. Today, Jesus Christ lives and works among us through the Holy Spirit. Jesus said, "I have told you this, so that when the time comes you will remember that I warned you. I did not tell you this at first because I was with you" (John 16:4). The Holy Spirit teaches and guides us for the glory of God. Where the Holy Spirit resides, Jesus Christ is present. Being filled with the Holy Spirit—acknowledging, welcoming and accepting the Holy Spirit—is the same as being filled with Jesus Christ.

After Christ's ascension, one hundred twenty of His disciples earnestly prayed with one heart. As they were praying, a great sound as of a rushing wind came from heaven and, like tongues of fire, rested on the head of every man. Then each man was filled with the Holy Spirit, and the Holy Spirit empowered them to speak in tongues of different lands.

The followers filled with the Spirit were also filled with confidence. They began to boldly witness to the gospel. Wherever they went, God's miracles were manifest; the cripples began to walk, the dead began to rise again, and evil spirits were driven out of people. As a result, Christianity was spread through the Roman Empire in less than three hundred years.

When we are filled with the Holy Spirit, we experience Jesus Christ in our hearts and are filled with Him. The gospel of Jesus Christ is not some ethical rule or some philosophy. As the Son of the living God, Jesus Christ saves us and gives us freedom and life.

FILLED WITH THE BIBLE

If we disregard and ignore God's Word, we cannot discover Jesus Christ. Jesus is the Word. John 1:1 says, "In the beginning was the Word, and the Word was with God, and the Word was God." Because God works through His Word, you cannot experience the miraculous work of Jesus Christ without the Word—no matter how diligently you come to church to worship. We shouldn't wander here and there hoping to find Christ, but we must be filled with the Holy Spirit. When we are filled with the Holy Spirit, we will also realize that Jesus Christ lives in our hearts. As we understand the Bible, we gain an understanding of Jesus Christ and His ministry. But trying to live a life of faith without the Word is like setting off on a long journey without a map. In order for us to stop our wandering and despairing, we must live with God's Word.

FILLED WITH FAITH

No matter how much a person is filled with the Holy Spirit, if he does not believe in the Bible, he will not be able to accomplish anything.

**I pray that out of his glorious riches he may
strengthen you with power through his Spirit
in your inner being, so that Christ may dwell
in your hearts through faith. And I pray that
you, being rooted and established in love, may
have power.**
—EPHESIANS 3:16–18

Faith is believing that the living God bestows a great gift of life to those who seek after Him. Faith can only be granted by God. In order for us to receive this faith from God, there is a conscious decision on our part. Our decision becomes the starting point for our faith.

Some people say they will believe in God after they have mastered the Bible, experienced various fulfillments and have their wishes accomplished. This is a false faith. Faith is granted to us when we decide to believe in Jesus Christ despite our ignorance or our lack of experiencing the fulfillment of the Holy Spirit.

We must first decide to believe in God. When we show such desire, God leads us to the truth step by step. As we understand the Bible more and more, we shall experience the fulfillment of the Holy Spirit, and our faith will increase. When we live in faith, we can experience the life of Jesus Christ.

THE BLESSINGS OF THE SON'S LEGACY

People live dreary and desolate lives and are unable to find refuge and peace. Although they search, refuge is not possible for them. Only Jesus Christ, who died for mankind, can lead us to green pastures. In Him we find a refuge and a resting place for our souls and bodies. Jesus said, "I am the good shepherd. The good shepherd lays down his life for the sheep" (John 10:11). Jesus Christ, the Good Shepherd, makes His presence known among us as the Holy Spirit, and He leads us to the cross. It is under the cross where we find Christ's own pasture.

What are the blessings that we can experience and receive under the cross of Jesus Christ?

FORGIVENESS

People are unable to attain peace of the mind and heart because they are unable to break free from their guilt. For us to break free from guilt, we must come before the cross and repent of our sins. Repentance is not merely realizing that we have sinned, but repentance means stopping ourselves from committing the sins again. As we repent of our sins and are forgiven, we can have peace. Jesus not only cleared the debts of our past and present, but He cleared the debt of our future as well.

RECONCILIATION

There is a pasture of reconciliation under the cross. For many generations, mankind has been God's enemy. Ever since the sin of Adam and Eve, the relationship between God and man has been severed; man lives in fear of the judgment of God.

Jesus Christ came into this world and restored the relationship between man and God by being judged on the cross in our place. All who come before the cross are given the blessing of living in harmony and in fellowship with God.

All this is from God, who reconciled us to himself through Christ and gave us the ministry of reconciliation: that God was reconciling the world to himself in Christ, not counting men's sins against them. And he has committed to us the message of reconciliation.
—2 CORINTHIANS 5:18–19

Not only are we reconciled with God, but we can also live in harmony with our neighbors. Paul wrote that living in harmony with our neighbors is the will of God. (See 1 Thessalonians 5:13.) Man cannot live alone as a hermit. He must live in peace and harmony with his neighbors. Through Jesus Christ, we find peace with God, and we further extend that peace and harmony to our neighbors. A person who has peace with God will find peace with his neighbors, and with this peace and harmony, he can find happiness.

HEALING

Every institution of society suffers from an illness. The spiritual life, the heart, the body and the daily life of every man have been affected by this illness. The illness has affected our families, societies, countries and the world.

Man is suffering from this illness because he has distanced himself from God and does not know where he came from, why he is living or where he is headed. The anxiety results in denial, uncertainty and violence, which causes our families, societies and nations to become ill.

We must come under the cross of Jesus Christ and receive the healing of our spirits, hearts and bodies. Families on the verge of disunity because of quarrels and problems must come under the cross of Jesus Christ to be healed. The only way for a country and a people to be healed of its illnesses is through the cross of Jesus Christ.

FREEDOM FROM DAMNATION

The cross is the origin of all blessings. God does not wish to see a believer in Christ bound by curses and shivering from hunger and cold. His Word tells us, "Ask and it shall be given to you; seek and you will find; knock and the door will be opened to you" (Matt. 7:7). We must not be bound by poverty or damnation, but instead, we must seek and knock on God's door so that we may receive the blessings that are inherent in the cross. Once blessed, we are called to help others.

HOPE OF HEAVEN

A man is like a pilgrim. He is on a journey and will not live forever. He must leave this life. When we leave this world, those who accepted Christ shall receive everlasting life, but those who didn't shall receive eternal punishment. The Bible says, "For the message of the cross is foolishness to those who are perishing, but to us who are being saved it is the power of God" (1 Cor. 1:18).

Those who wish to obtain everlasting life must come to Christ and come under the cross. Those under the cross shall be resurrected in glory on the day of Christ's Second Coming, and they will receive everlasting life and dwell with God forever. Under Christ's cross, there is true forgiveness and reconciliation, healing and blessing, and the hope of eternal paradise. Jesus Christ, the Good Shepherd, has led us to the cross so that we may be blessed.

Dear almighty God, we thank You for giving us Christ's name, which has power and authority. Help us to experience the life of Jesus Christ in our daily lives by filling us with the Holy Spirit, filling us with Your Word and filling us with faith. We thank You for leading us to the green pastures of peace and rest. Help us to live within Your grace and blessing under the cross until the day we enter into heaven. In Jesus' name, amen.

Part Three
God the Holy Spirit

TWELVE

The Personality of the Holy Spirit

About two thousand years ago, Jesus Christ died on the cross to redeem the sins of all mankind. He was resurrected and ascended to heaven. Although He is no longer in this world physically, Jesus Christ made a promise to be with us always: "And surely I am with you always, to the very end of the age" (Matt. 28:20). How is He with us today? Through the person of the Holy Spirit, the third Person of the triune God. Who is the Holy Spirit?

THE SPIRIT OF JESUS CHRIST

Because of His prior knowledge of the future, Jesus was able to tell His disciples about events that would follow (Matt. 16:21). He told them He would bear the sins of all mankind and die on the cross. Then three days after His death, He would be resurrected.

The disciples who heard Christ were filled with despair and sadness. They didn't know what to do. Having left their parents, brothers and relatives, they had followed Christ and depended on Him completely. With Christ's warning the disciples began to fear for the future. They must have felt like orphans left out in the world to fend for themselves. Seeing their faces, Jesus Christ understood their fears and gave them words of comfort.

And I will ask the Father, and he will give you another Counselor to be with you forever—the Spirit of truth. The world cannot accept him, because it neither sees him nor knows him. But you know him, for he lives with you and will be in you.
—JOHN 14:16–17

Just as Jesus had promised, the Holy Spirit descended on the disciples on the Day of Pentecost. Although they were like lost orphans, because of the presence of the Holy Spirit in their hearts, their inner beings were filled with God's presence. As such, they became powerful witnesses as they boldly spread the gospel.

The Holy Spirit makes His presence known among us, comforts us in our fear and despair and transforms us into bold Christians.

THE GOSPEL-WITNESSING SPIRIT

After Adam and Eve disobeyed God, the spirits of men were severed from God. Jesus came to this world to save mankind. By bearing sin, condemnation and death, Jesus Christ tore down the wall that stood between God and man. Through what Christ has done, we have received salvation, found peace with God and received everlasting life. "When the Counselor comes, whom I will send to you from the Father, the Spirit of truth who goes out from the Father, he will testify about me" (John 15:26). Just as Christ had predicted, the Holy Spirit is, even now, fulfilling His role as a witness for the gospel of Jesus Christ.

Before receiving the Holy Spirit, Peter denied knowing Christ three times. His faith in Jesus Christ lacked conviction. However, after he received the Holy Spirit, he stood boldly to proclaim the gospel—and three thousand people received Christ in a single day.

The worries we have in this life concerning what to eat, drink or wear are temporary; however, at death all of these cares melt away like snow on a spring day. Then we must face the most important decision of where our spirits will go. If our spirits belong to God, we receive eternal life. If not, we suffer forever in hell. The most important matter is the salvation of our souls and our brother. We must accept the Holy Spirit, and we must spread the gospel to all people.

THE SPIRIT
OF HEALING

After Adam and Eve betrayed God, the bodies and hearts of men became ill with disease affecting both families and societies. However, when we accept Christ as our Savior and allow the Holy Spirit to come into our hearts, the healing of spirit takes place.

Earlier I mentioned the story of a crippled man being healed in Acts 3:1-10. As Peter and John were going to the temple for prayer, there was a man who was crippled from birth begging for alms. Peter and John said to the crippled man, "Look at us." The crippled man looked up at Peter and John, hoping they would give him money. However, Peter spoke that which may have been beyond what the crippled man could have expected. "Silver and gold I do not have...stand in the name of Jesus Christ . . . " While speaking these words, Peter took the right hand of the crippled man and pulled him up. Just then, the legs and the ankles of the crippled man began to grow stronger, and he began to walk, jump and praise God.

Today, many people are crippled spiritually and physically. They limp through their lives as cripples. The Holy Spirit came as a healer; He wants to heal us, and through us He wants to heal others.

THE EVANGELICAL SPIRIT

Before Christ's ascension to heaven, He commanded His disciples to be His witnesses and to engage in the ministry of evangelism. "But you will receive power when the Holy Spirit comes on you; and you will be my witnesses in Jerusalem, and in all Judea and Samaria, and to the ends of the earth" (Acts 1:8). To fulfill this mission, we must be filled with the Holy Spirit and utilize His power and authority. As Jerusalem burned with the fire of the Holy Spirit, the gospel rode on top of the flames and was spread to Judea and Samaria. The gospel continued to be spread even when faced with severe persecution, accomplishing the great task of evangelizing the Roman Empire within three hundred years. The gospel was able to spread so far and so quickly because there was the power and the authority of the Holy Spirit.

Not only does the Holy Spirit give authority and power to those who are witnesses of the gospel, He also guides us. When we look at the Bible, we discover how God prepared the way for all nations to hear the gospel by having the Holy Spirit guide Paul's steps (Acts 16:6–10). On his second mission of evangelism, Paul tried to follow his own judgment to preach the gospel in Asia. However, the Holy Spirit did not allow Paul to do so. Paul saw a vision in the night. He saw a Macedonian asking him to "help those of us in Macedonia."

Upon seeing this vision, Paul changed his direction and headed for Macedonia.

As a result, the gospel moved from Palestine to Rome, from Rome to Germany, from Germany to England and from England to America. Today, the gospel has reached Asia. Even now the Holy Spirit is moving about and doing miraculous works in Asia. The Holy Spirit is calling for those of us who will listen to engage in this the last harvest.

Farmers plant the rice seeds in seedbeds. After sprouting, the sprouts are transplanted to another field. The role of the seedbed is very important. Among the Asian nations, Korea—our very country—has become the seedbed for the gospel. Among the three billion people living throughout Asia, there is not a country where the work of the Holy Spirit is greater than in Korea. We can see the great work of the Holy Spirit when we count the overwhelming number of churches and Christians in Korea and compare them to any other Asian country.

God has made our country a seedbed for the gospel and turned our country into a great Christian nation. We must realize that we are entrusted with the mission of going to every nation of the world to plant the seeds of the gospel, and we must be strengthened by the Holy Spirit to accomplish our mission. The Holy Spirit is the Spirit of Jesus Christ, the Spirit of the gospel, the Spirit of healing and the Spirit of evangelism. We must abide in the Holy Spirit so that these great works become manifest.

THE HOLY SPIRIT IS THE SPIRIT OF GOD

Despite their having seen and having met the resurrected Christ, the disciples were not able to spread the gospel until they had received the Holy Spirit. Prior to having received the Holy Spirit, they were fearful and hid themselves. Once they received the Holy Spirit, they ran out into the open to spread the gospel. As a result, many wonderful miracles occurred. A great number of sinners were saved, sick persons were healed, and evil spirits were driven out.

Such an incredible transformation is only possible through the work of the Holy Spirit. The help of the Holy Spirit is an absolute necessity for the person who desires power. Also the growth of the church is made possible through the Holy Spirit. How does the Holy Spirit cause such changes and miracles?

THE WISDOM AND INTELLIGENCE OF THE HOLY SPIRIT

After the death of Jesus Christ the disciples were overcome. They had followed Jesus Christ for three and a half years, received teaching about faith and trained as disciples. They were mired in despair. They did not fully understand the meaning of Christ's suffering, resurrection and His ascension. They didn't realize that through Christ's redemption on the cross, the sins of mankind were cleansed and that God's great plan for man's salvation was complete. They believed Jesus to be the Messiah who had come to return Israel's sovereignty and release the Israelites from the grips of the Romans.

Today, many people misunderstand the meaning of redemption, and being bound by humanistic views, they believe Christ's gospel of the kingdom of heaven to be some ideology much like the ideas of democracy and communism. The reason for their blindness is because they do not have within them the Holy Spirit. They continue to suffer under the burden of sin, disease, condemnation and death.

Why is it that they cannot fully understand the meaning of the cross? The full implication of the cross is a hidden secret of God that can only be understood through the help of the Holy Spirit. Only after the disciples had received the Holy Spirit did they understand that the death of Christ was a redemption that cleared all man's debts.

With this realization, the disciples were able to become bold witnesses. We must be filled with the Spirit so that the Holy Spirit can impart to us the wisdom to understand the truth about God's kingdom.

THE SPIRIT OF SCHEMES AND TALENTS

The meaning of the word *scheme* is "a plan of action to find a solution for the problem." The disciples of Christ were all either fishermen or tax collectors. They lacked formal education. However, after they received the Holy Spirit, they were filled with schemes and gifts of the mind. After Peter and John were filled with the Holy Spirit, they boldly faced the elders and the public officials of the people to preach the gospel. Many people who saw them thought it a strange sight. "When they saw the courage of Peter and John and realized that they were unschooled, ordinary men, they were astonished and they took note that these men had been with Jesus" (Acts 4:13).

The Holy Spirit is a spirit of schemes and abilities. Wherever the gospel is proclaimed, the Holy Spirit drives away ignorance and myths. In their place civilization begins to flourish. When we look at the countries where culture has flourished, we can observe that the gospel has been accepted in those countries. If the gospel of Jesus Christ had not reached Europe and America, the focus on Western culture would not exist today. When this spirit of schemes and ideas abides with us, we can brush aside Satan's plots and live in victory.

THE SPIRIT OF KNOWLEDGE AND THE FEAR OF GOD

Through the Holy Spirit we obtain greater knowledge about God. The knowledge that the Holy Spirit gives us is not some academic knowledge, but rather, it is a revelatory knowledge through the Bible. God transcends the capability of mankind to understand. We simply cannot accurately understand God with our natural minds. Disregarding this shortfall, if a man tries to learn about God through academically based research, he may only find himself turning his back on God.

If we desire knowledge about God, we must first repent and, with faith in Jesus Christ, be filled with the Holy Spirit. The Holy Spirit knows all things, even the deeper things of God. The only way for us to understand God is by being filled with the Holy Spirit. (See 1 Corinthians 2:10.)

Jesus asked His disciples one day, "Who do you say I am?" (Matt. 16:15).

Peter responded, "You are the Christ, the son of the living God" (v. 16). Peter was able to confess such words of faith because through the Holy Spirit, God made it possible for Peter to understand God's wisdom and secrets.

The Holy Spirit puts fear and respect in our hearts so that we may offer righteous worship to God. The psalmist said, "Serve the LORD with fear and rejoice with trembling" (Ps. 2:11). Paul said, "Therefore, my dear friends, as you have always obeyed—not only in my presence, but now much more in my absence—continue to work out your salvation with fear and trembling" (Phil. 2:12). God is not to be taken lightly, but should be worshiped with fear and trembling. The Holy Spirit makes it possible for us to have the fear of God.

In these ways, the Holy Spirit gives us knowledge about God so that we may offer a righteous worship with fear and

146

respect. Whenever we read the Bible, pray or do anything at all, we must trust the Holy Spirit to give us the knowledge and fear of God.

THE SPIRIT OF CHARACTER

A man's character is very important. People respect and envy the person whom they believe to have character.

God also has character. However, because the Holy Spirit is often referred to as "the firelike Spirit," "the windlike Spirit," the dovelike Spirit," for example, many people fail to realize that the Holy Spirit is the *living* Holy Spirit. The Holy Spirit is a Spirit with "character." As the Holy Spirit does indeed have character, we must not ignore Him.

THE SPIRIT WHO HAS KNOWLEDGE

The Holy Spirit has all knowledge. The Bible attests to this fact.

However, as it is written: "No eye has seen, no ear has heard, no mind has conceived what God has prepared for those who love him"—but God has revealed it to us by his Spirit.
—1 Corinthians 2:9–10

The Holy Spirit is one with God and shares God's knowledge. Also, the Bible says, "For who among men knows the thoughts of a man except the man's spirit within him? In the same way no one knows the thoughts of God except the Spirit of God" (1 Cor. 2:11). The Holy Spirit is a Spirit of knowledge who not only knows all things that God knows, but also has complete knowledge about mankind.

THE SPIRIT
WHO HAS EMOTIONS

The Holy Spirit has emotions. When we ignore God's will and disobey God, the Holy Spirit is saddened. The Bible advises us not to cause sadness to the Holy Spirit. "And do not grieve the Holy Spirit of God, with whom you were sealed for the day of redemption" (Eph. 4:30).

The Bible also warns us about the wrath of the Holy Spirit. "Today, if you hear his voice, do not harden your hearts as you did in the rebellion, during the time of testing in the desert" (Heb. 3:7–8). The Holy Spirit has emotions.

THE SPIRIT
WHO HAS A WILL

In addition to knowledge and emotions, the Holy Spirit has a will and determination. "All these are the work of one and the same Spirit, and he gives them to each one, just as he determines" (1 Cor. 12:11). We pray to God and ask for His blessings, but we cannot receive the blessings according to our own wishes. The Holy Spirit grants us these blessings according to His will.

Aside from this, the Holy Spirit, with unbreakable determination, teaches us, helps us to remember, watches over us and leads us. The Holy Spirit not only makes us holy, but He also enables us and strengthens our faith.

The Holy Spirit works among us with determination to become our helper, our teacher, our defender, our guide and our comforter—and He desires communication with us.

THE SPIRIT WHO
DESIRES COMMUNICATION

If communication is severed between people, their relationship breaks down. For our families and neighbors to become closer and share meaningful lives, there must be continued communication. Similarly, for us to have personal relationships with the Holy Spirit, there must be continued communication.

The word *communication* in the phrase "communication with the Holy Spirit" is *koinonia*. In Greek the word *koinonia* means "fellowship." Because the Holy Spirit is the personification of God, if we do not communicate with God and continue in fellowship with the Holy Spirit, our faith will gradually wither. Only when the Holy Spirit fills our hearts with God's love and grace can we understand that love and grace allow us to have a burning faith. Therefore, we must continually communicate with the Holy Spirit.

To communicate and fellowship with God, we must pray. Whenever I prepare to deliver God's message, I pray, "O Holy Spirit, please be with me, for I am inadequate." When I lead a revival meeting abroad where the language and culture are different, I depend and trust the Holy Spirit more earnestly. The Holy Spirit helps me. This is because through my prayer, there is a fellowship between the Holy Spirit and me. The Holy Spirit helps us to lead successful and victorious lives. How much communication we have with the Holy Spirit is a gauge of how successful we are in living by faith.

Communication with the Holy Spirit also refers to a "partnership." The Holy Spirit is our partner for life as well as a partner in our work for God's kingdom. As a partner, the Holy Spirit wishes to be a part of every aspect of our lives. When we give our lives to the Holy Spirit and pray, the Holy Spirit guides us with dreams, visions, knowledge and wisdom. Without His guidance we cannot successfully perform God's work.

The Holy Spirit stood in Paul's way when he decided on his own to go to Asia to preach the gospel. As he tried to go to Bithynia, he failed miserably to reach his destination. The Holy Spirit showed him a vision of a Macedonian who asked him, "Come to Macedonia and help us." Paul promptly went to Macedonia, preached the gospel there and laid the foundation for evangelization of Europe.

The Holy Spirit came to work among us because He desires to become our partner. When we work in partnership with the Holy Spirit, we may feel at times that we are losing out on the partnership. But when we look at the result of that partnership, we will realize that there is great victory for us. We must accept Him as our partner and fulfill the duties given us by Jesus Christ.

Communication with the Holy Spirit also means "oneness." The Holy Spirit ties all of us with Christ's bond of love to become one with Christ. Slander and disintegration are the methods of Satan. The work of the Holy Spirit motivates families, workplaces, even churches and church districts to be one in love and harmony. Slandering and attacking are the works of the devil. Paul wrote, *"All* the saints send their greetings" (2 Cor. 13:13, emphasis added).

The Holy Spirit has intelligence, emotions and righteousness. He is with us even now, and He desires fellowship with us. As we live with the Holy Spirit, we will be filled with dreams and hopes.

O living God, we acknowledge, welcome, accept and trust the Holy Spirit who does great work as He abides in us. Fill us with the Holy Spirit this very moment, and help us so that our lives can glorify Your name. Help us to live in continued fellowship with the Holy Spirit so that we may live victoriously from now until the day we enter heaven. In Christ's name, amen.

THIRTEEN

The Work of the Holy Spirit

n Genesis we read that God created "existence" from "nonexistence." Before God's work in creating this world, there was confusion and emptiness, a void filled with complete darkness. The Bible says, "Now the earth was formless and empty, darkness was over the surface of the deep, and the Spirit of God was hovering over the waters" (Gen. 1:2). As a hen sits and nurtures her eggs by warming them, the Holy Spirit nurtured this chaotic state. As the chaos was nurtured by the Holy Spirit, the Word of God was added to the chaos. This combination caused the creation of "existence" from "nonexistence." From this we can clearly see that the Holy Spirit works through God's Word.

THE HOLY SPIRIT AND THE WORD

The Holy Spirit and the Word of God were partners in the creation of the world. The Bible says, "In the beginning was the Word, and the Word was with God, and the Word was God . . . The Word became flesh and made his dwelling among us" (John 1:1, 14).

Jesus was the physical manifestation of the Word of God, but He did not enter into His ministry of salvation before He was baptized by John the Baptist in the Jordan River. Only after Jesus was baptized in the river and the Holy Spirit, like a dove, descended on His head, did He begin on His ministry as the Savior of mankind. With the Holy Spirit, Jesus Christ drove out evil spirits, healed many illnesses, raised the dead and did many other miracles.

The disciples of Christ performed miracles when they were filled with the Holy Spirit and the Word. Because they followed Christ for three and a half years, they were filled with Christ's teaching, the Word. However, they became capable of great things only after they were filled with the Holy Spirit. As the Holy Spirit descended on them, the followers received authority and power.

It was the Holy Spirit who made it possible for Peter to go out and cause three thousand people to repent and be baptized through his witnessing. The Holy Spirit made it possible for Peter and John to miraculously make the cripple walk with the words, "Silver and gold I do not have, but what I have I give you. In the name of Jesus Christ of Nazareth, walk" (Acts 3:6). The Holy Spirit does miracles through words, not unlike the miracle of Creation.

THE HOLY SPIRIT AND US

The Holy Spirit works for us unceasingly. In the Old Testament, the Spirit of God descended only on the high priests, prophets or kings. In the New Testament era, the Spirit of God worked with Jesus Christ, and after Christ's ascension, the Holy Spirit descended on the one hundred twenty followers. Today, the Holy Spirit descends on all those who repent of their sins and believe in Jesus Christ.

To experience the works of the Holy Spirit, we must accept and revere Him. If we were to look down upon or deny the existence of the Holy Spirit, He would be grieved. Should the Holy Spirit be grieved, we will not be able to experience His miraculous works. We must live acknowledging, greeting, accepting and trusting the Holy Spirit.

Living in faith is a life managed and led by the Holy Spirit. Without the Holy Spirit, we cannot receive Jesus Christ as our Savior, nor can we offer true prayer, praise or worship.

A person who does not have the Holy Spirit lives with superficial faith. We must be filled with the Holy Spirit so that we can experience great world-shaking miracles.

The Holy Spirit is poured out on those who believe in Jesus Christ. Despite what God does for us, the reason that we cannot experience the works of the Holy Spirit is because we do not trust in Christ, read the Bible and pray. When we become filled with the Holy Spirit through reading the Bible and praying to God, we shall experience great miracles.

Another reason we cannot experience the miracles of the Holy Spirit is that we prevent the Him from doing His work by not presenting Him with the Word within us and because we fail to declare our faith in Jesus Christ. To experience the miracles of the Holy Spirit, we must believe in the Word, and we must declare our faith in Jesus Christ.

When we are suffering from illnesses and desire God's divine healing, we must call out to God with words of faith: "I have found harmony with God though the blood of Jesus Christ, and through the work of the Holy Spirit I have been made righteous. Christ has taken charge of all my illnesses because He is aware of my weaknesses. By having His body broken, Jesus Christ has healed me." When we declare our faith in such a way, the Holy Spirit hears those words and heals us according to our confession of faith. This does not mean that we should confess our faith like a parrot speaking words it does not understand. What it means is that after you have declared these words, you must wait expectantly for the healing that the Holy Spirit brings. "Through Christ's wounds, I have been healed." When we thusly declare our faith, we shall experience the work of the Holy Spirit.

When we face situations that are real and immediate, such as hunger due to poverty or failure in life, we must depend on the Word of God so that the Holy Spirit can descend over the situation and bring to us well-being. The importance of our declaration of faith in God's Word cannot be stressed enough. Jesus said, "I will give you the keys of the kingdom of heaven; whatever you bind on earth will be bound in heaven, and whatever you loose on earth will be loosed in heaven" (Matt. 16:19). Based upon our declaration of faith, the Holy Spirit works to show us the miracles of God. With our dependence on the Holy Spirit, who works according to the Word of God, we must declare our words of optimism and creativity. When we do this, the Holy Spirit brings new order, gives new life and fills us with abundance.

THE HOLY SPIRIT AND THE LAW

Wherever people gather to form a society, there must be law and order. As each person has different views on life as well as different goals, they must agree on a common set of laws.

However, regulations and laws that are made by mankind cannot be complete or perfect. Only the omnipotent God has the perfect and absolute law. God gave the Ten Commandments to the Israelites. However, there were none who could comply with God's commandments. This is the reason why, in order to fulfill the Law, Jesus Christ died on the cross in our place. Jesus Christ gave us the new law of the Holy Spirit. What is the law of the Holy Spirit?

THE LAW OF THE NEW ERA

In the Old Testament, there were many laws based on the Ten Commandments that were given through Moses. Although God gave the Israelites the Law, there was not a single person who was able to keep the all aspects of the Law completely. As a result, everyone was placed under judgment.

Jesus Christ came to the world to fulfill the Law and open the new era of blessings. By suffering on the cross, Jesus cleared all the debts of our past, present and future, and He saved us from the judgment of the Law. Just as new laws are made when a new era comes to rule, in this period of grace, the authority of the Law of Moses has given way to the law of the Holy Spirit of love.

THE LAW OF FORGIVENESS AND LOVE

In John 8:1–11 we see a woman who was caught while in the act of committing adultery. The Law of Moses condemned her. She was brought to Jesus. A person from the crowd boldly asked Jesus a question. "Teacher, this woman was caught in the act of adultery. In the Law Moses commanded us to stone such women. Now what do you say?" (vv. 4–5).

Jesus stooped down and wrote something on the ground in silence, and then He spoke. "If any one of you is without sin, let him be the first to throw a stone at her" (v. 7). Hearing Christ's words, each person in the crowd began to realize their own sins. A short time later Jesus met the woman and said to her, "Neither do I condemn you of your sin. Go and do not sin."

According to the commandments given to Moses, the woman deserved death by stoning. However, the law of life freed her from being judged under the law of sin and death. Anyone who believes in Jesus Christ will not be punished by the Law of Moses, but will experience forgiveness.

THE LAW OF GRACE AND TRUTH

**For the law was given through Moses; grace
and truth came through Jesus Christ.**
–JOHN 1:17

After Jesus Christ came to this world, the era of the Law of Moses was superseded by the law of the Holy Spirit.

The famous evangelist D. L. Moody was preparing a sermon on grace. While preparing the sermon, he was overcome with emotions as he was blessed with God's grace, and he ran out to the streets. He grabbed a police officer who happened to be passing by and asked him a question, "Do you know what grace is?" The police officer was moved by Moody's question, causing him to repent of his sins and accept Jesus Christ. The grace of God moves people emotionally. If we have received salvation through Jesus Christ, we must seek after truth and knowledge. Jesus said, "I have spoken to you of earthly things and you do not believe; how then will you believe if I speak of heavenly things?" (John 3:12).

Those who do not know the truth are still bound by the Law and live in frustration and despair. Those who believe in Jesus Christ as the way, the truth, and the life live in devotion while seeking after the truth. This is made possible by the Holy Spirit who comes into us to clean away immorality and vileness. The law of the Holy Spirit is the law of the new era, the law of forgiveness and the law of grace and truth. We have been made anew and live under this law of the Holy Spirit of life.

THE WORK OF THE HOLY SPIRIT

All of us on earth live according to the natural laws of existence. For example, herbivorous animals eat vegetables, and carnivorous animals eat the herbivores. When the carnivores die, the bacteria break down and absorb into the bodies of the carnivores. There is an endless cycle, or chain, of death and renewal. As long as the cycle continues to work, life on earth continues. Aside from this one example, there are many other laws of renewal.

In order for the church, which is the body of Jesus Christ, to continue to survive in health, the church must also continually take part in spiritual renewal with the Holy Spirit.

Someone who says, "Life in Christ is good either with or without the Holy Spirit," misunderstands the basic truth of the Christian faith. A Christian who has not received the Holy Spirit can only understand the theoretical, philosophical and moral principles while failing to understand the life of faith.

Righteous living in Christian faith is a life in harmony with the Holy Spirit. To live in such harmony, we must first acknowledge, greet and accept the Holy Spirit in our hearts. Only then can gratitude and praise spring forth from our hearts. What does the Holy Spirit do within us?

THE HOLY SPIRIT REPROACHES THE WORLD.

Jesus Christ was clear concerning the work of the Holy Spirit. "When he comes, he will convict the world of guilt in regard to sin and righteousness and judgment" (John 16:8).

First, the Holy Spirit reproaches the world for its sin. The Holy Spirit will convict our hearts so that we realize our sins. People commit sin both knowingly and in ignorance. Of all the sins that people commit, the worst sin is that of rejecting Jesus Christ. Jesus Christ gave up heaven and came to earth for sinful mankind who deserved to be condemned. Jesus Christ then died on the cross to take away our sins. If we do not believe in Jesus Christ, we cannot avoid God's judgment.

Second, the Holy Spirit reproaches the world concerning righteousness. Since the beginning of mankind's existence, countless people have been born and died in this world, but there is no one (besides Enoch and Elijah) who has escaped death (Gen. 5:24; 2 Kings 2:11). However, Jesus Christ was resurrected three days after His death. Christ's resurrection means that all the debts of mankind have been cleared, and at the same time, a way to salvation and righteousness has been opened. The Holy Spirit helps us to realize this essential fact.

Third, the Holy Spirit helps us to realize that Satan, who had been acting as the king of this world, has been judged. The reason that Satan was able to act as the king of this world was because man had betrayed God and walked down the path of sin. By Christ's cleansing of our sins with His own blood, Satan was denied this role as king of this world. For those of us who believe in Christ, we have been freed from the law of death and sin, and now we live in freedom under the law of the Holy Spirit of love. The Holy Spirit helps us to realize this fact.

THE HOLY SPIRIT HELPS US TO ACCEPT JESUS CHRIST AS SAVIOR.

The Holy Spirit makes it possible for us to look to Christ and accept Him as our Savior. Through our rationality and intelligence it is impossible for us to believe that Christ died for our sins and was resurrected. The Holy Spirit gives us the understanding to overcome the limitation of our minds.

Therefore I tell you that no one who is speaking by the Spirit of God says, "Jesus be cursed," and no one can say, "Jesus is Lord," except by the Holy Spirit.

—1 CORINTHIANS 12:3

THE HOLY SPIRIT GIVES US POWER.

Living by faith is a continual spiritual battle. Peter warned, "Be self-controlled and alert. Your enemy the devil prowls around like a roaring lion looking for someone to devour. Resist him, standing firm in the faith, because you know that your brothers throughout the world are undergoing the same kind of sufferings" (1 Pet. 5:8–9).

How can we be victorious over Satan's temptation? The Bible teaches us the way to victory.

Therefore put on the full armor of God, so that when the day of evil comes, you may be able to stand your ground, and after you have done everything, to stand. Stand firm then, with the belt of truth buckled around your waist, with the breastplate of righteousness in place, and

with your feet fitted with the readiness that
comes from the gospel of peace. In addition to
all this, take up the shield of faith, with which
you can extinguish all the flaming arrows of the
evil one. Take the helmet of salvation and the
sword of the Spirit, which is the word of God.
—EPHESIANS 6:13–17

If we were not given the authority of the Holy Spirit, we would not only fail in our spiritual life, but we would also not do any work for God. We must ask God for the power of the Holy Spirit. With the power of the Holy Spirit, we will be victorious in all our confrontation with Satan, and we will experience the hand of God. The Holy Spirit reproaches this world, enables us to believe in Jesus Christ and gives us strength and power to do God's work. When we are helped by the Holy Spirit, we can live victoriously.

THE HOLY SPIRIT STRENGTHENS OUR WEAKNESSES.

When people feel that their work is important, they become eager and determined and are able to overcome difficulties. However, when people are overcome with the thought that their work is useless or in vain, they are overcome with anxiety and fretfulness. They easily abandon their work. At times, even Christians find themselves in a state of dejection.

The Bible teaches us about overcoming a state of weakness and dejection. "And we know that in all things God works for the good of those who love him, who have been called according to his purpose" (Rom. 8:28). When we love God and have been called according to His purpose, the Holy Spirit works for us and in us.

THE HOLY SPIRIT AND THE BELIEVER

The Holy Spirit can easily change our environment as well as our destiny. However, He does not offer His help to everyone. How can we be confident that we have the help of the Holy Spirit?

THE BELIEVER WHO LOVES GOD

If we love God, the Holy Spirit grants us ability and power.

What does the love of God mean? All people like to spend as much time as possible with people they love. When we confess love to another, but have our hearts and minds elsewhere, our confessions are empty words. With true lovers, even though their physical bodies may be far apart, their hearts are always together spiritually. Such closeness makes it possible for heart-to-heart communication even from a distance. Loving God is the same. It is having our hearts pointed toward God. We cannot be satisfied with only praising and thanking God in worship services on Sundays. Having love for God means communicating with God continuously.

Jesus said, "Yet a time is coming and has now come when the true worshipers will worship the Father in spirit and truth, for they are the kind of worshipers the Father seeks. God is spirit, and his worshipers must worship in spirit and in truth" (John 4:23–24). To love God is to have reverence and sincerity toward God.

THE BELIEVER WHO PROCLAIMS THE GOSPEL

When we love someone, we tend to see only the good qualities in that person. Wherever we go, we boast and talk about that person. Parents who love their children look upon even their misdeeds with love. They try to cover their faults and boast about their children to their neighbors. The wife who loves her husband will boast about her husband to others. A husband who loves his wife will not expose her faults to others, but only talk about her merits. If we love God, we will have an intense desire to talk about His goodness and His Son, Jesus Christ.

God is truly good. He is the almighty God who created the universe and all things in it. He is the source of all blessings. God sent to this world His only begotten Son, Jesus Christ, because of His love for mankind. And by having Jesus Christ responsible for all our sins, God has opened the path to salvation and eternal life for anyone who believes in Jesus Christ. God has also sent us the Holy Spirit so that the Holy Spirit can help us with our weaknesses. How can we who confess love for God not proclaim the gospel?

When we truly love God we will spread the gospel. The Holy Spirit gives us power to carry out our work. Paul confessed, "Yet when I preach the gospel, I cannot boast, for I am compelled to preach. Woe to me if I do not preach the gospel!" (1 Cor. 9:16). The Holy Spirit helped Paul to spread the gospel and helped him overcome his weaknesses. As Christians, we must devote ourselves to proclaiming and spreading the gospel. Only then can we experience the helping hand of the Holy Spirit.

THE BELIEVER WHO PLEASES GOD

We will go to any length to make the person we love happy. Confessing to having the desire to please a person but not making a true effort to do so is a sign of insincere love. Children who love their parents try their best to make their parents happy; parents who love their children will sacrifice for them. If a person loves his country, he will give his life for his country.

If we love God, we must not hold ourselves back when it comes to pleasing Him. We will not begrudge any hardship or sacrifice. In addition to worshiping God with reverence and sincerity, we will give our time and effort for God's work. We will show our love for God by giving our tithes and helping our neighbors. We will do whatever we can to please Him.

So if you faithfully obey the commands I am
giving you today—to love the LORD your God
and to serve him with all your heart and with
all your soul—then I will send rain on your
land in its season, both autumn and spring
rains, so that you may gather in your grain,
new wine and oil. I will provide grass in the
fields for your cattle, and you will eat and be
satisfied.

—DEUTERONOMY 11:13–15

When we live a life focused on pleasing God, the Holy Spirit strengthens our weaknesses and adds to our blessings. The shortest path to experiencing the Holy Spirit's helping hand is by living in love with God and proclaiming the gospel of Christ.

THE HOLY SPIRIT WHO GUIDES US

The Holy Spirit resides in those who believe to provide a proof that we have become God's children. He guides us so that we live according to God's will. Jesus Christ said, "And I will ask the Father, and he will give you another Counselor to be with you forever" (John 14:16). The apostle Paul wrote, "So I say, live by the Spirit, and you will not gratify the desires of the sinful nature" (Gal. 5:16). We must always depend upon and be led by the Holy Spirit.

GUIDANCE THROUGH INTELLIGENCE

Some people teach that for us to be guided by the Holy Spirit, we must discard our intellect and reason. This is a false theology that stresses the mysterious nature of the Holy Spirit.

Those qualities that constitute a man—intellect and reason—help us to make judgments and decisions, to understand and to seek to investigate. The development of today's culture was made possible through the intellect and reason that God gave to mankind. However, mankind has come to believe that it was through his own strength and determination that civilization has developed. Man has become proud. Mankind has used his God-given intellect and reasoning to make weapons of war and to develop technology that destroys nature. These are not the purposes for which God gave mankind intellect and reason.

The intellect and reason that God has given mankind should be used to understand the wisdom of God.

But when he, the Spirit of truth, comes, he will guide you into all truth. He will not speak on his own; he will speak only what he hears, and he will tell you what is yet to come.
—JOHN 16:13

The only way we can understand the truth of God is if the Holy Spirit comes to help us. When the Holy Spirit enters into us and works in our intellect, we receive the wisdom to accomplish our work.

I read the testimony of a scientist published in a theological periodical. He was a physicist doing research on life. The research was not going anywhere, and he was discouraged. All of a sudden, a thought came to him, *Let me start again after a prayer.* He realized that in order for him to do research on the laws of nature that God had established, the first order of business was a prayer to God. He immediately knelt down on the floor of his research room and prayed earnestly for God to take charge of the research. Thereafter, the research progressed at an amazing pace, and he was able to submit his thesis. When the Holy Spirit is with us and guides us, we can accomplish work that seems impossible. The Holy Spirit has intellect. Paul wrote, "But God has revealed it to us by his Spirit" (1 Cor. 2:10). When the Holy Spirit provides us with His intellect, we can understand the living God.

GUIDANCE THROUGH EMOTION

The Holy Spirit has emotions and feelings. He plants God's love in our hearts so that we can act with emotions. He laments. The Bible says, "And do not grieve the Holy Spirit of God, with whom you were sealed for the day of redemption" (Eph. 4:30). And, "In the same way, the Spirit helps us in our weakness. We do not know what we ought to pray for, but the Spirit himself intercedes for us with groans that words cannot express" (Rom. 8:26).

The Holy Spirit guides us through our emotions. When we come to hope for something or have a wish in our hearts, we must first pray and ask for the Holy Spirit's guidance. When we pray for guidance about our hopes, and we are filled with uncertainty instead of being filled with peace and happiness, we must realize that this is a sign of the Holy Spirit's disapproval. "For it is God who works in you to will and to act according to his good purpose" (Phil. 2:13).

If it is something God wants, we are filled with burning desire as well as happiness, peace and certainty. We must first seek after the Holy Spirit's guidance and start on that work with peace, hope and certainty that the Holy Spirit gives to us.

GUIDANCE THROUGH WILL

The Holy Spirit has character, personality and a will. The Holy Spirit makes a judgment on whether our goals are that of God's will. If not, the Holy Spirit guides us so that our goals are in line with God. When we pursue after work that is not God's will, we face great obstacles that ultimately make us failures.

An example of this can be seen by looking at the first king of Israel. King Saul received God's command through the prophet Samuel to completely annihilate the Amalekites, not only the people but also all their livestock. However, Saul disobeyed God's command, and he took the king of Amalek as prisoner and spared all the healthy sheep and cows. Saul's disobedience angered God, and Saul was abandoned by God. Instead of repenting of his disobedience, Saul continued to live according to his own will in defiance of God, and he met a tragic end.

We must always submit to God's will.

We demolish arguments and every pretension that sets itself up against the knowledge of God, and we take captive every thought to make it obedient to Christ.
–2 CORINTHIANS 10:5

In his heart a man plans his course, but the LORD determines his steps.
–PROVERBS 16:9

We must always wait for the Holy Spirit's guidance and live according to what He tells us. The Holy Spirit, who has character and personality, leads us to God's will through our intellect, emotion and will.

O God of all creation, help us to experience great miracles in our lives as we depend on the Holy Spirit. Let us continually speak words of creativity and productivity. Help us to live with the blessing of salvation and live in hope under the law of the Holy Spirit of love with a true purpose in our lives. Help us to be filled with power through the Holy Spirit and be led by the Holy Spirit so that we can always make God happy and glorify Him. In Christ's name, amen.

FOURTEEN

The Baptism of the Holy Spirit

Jesus Christ emphasized the "coming of the Holy Spirit" to His disciples. Fufilling Christ's prophecy, fifty days after Christ's death the Holy Spirit descended on the one hundred twenty followers of Christ in the upper room as they prayed. And the Holy Spirit continues to do His work among Christians today.

WHEN THE HOLY SPIRIT APPEARED ON EARTH

How did the Holy Spirit descend on the Day of Pentecost on Christ's followers?

LIKE THE WIND

Suddenly a sound like the blowing of a violent wind came from heaven and filled the whole house where they were sitting.

—ACTS 2:2

There are reasons for the Holy Spirit being likened to wind.

First, when the Holy Spirit blows through us, all "dusty buildups" are swept away. A strong wind cleans the air. When a strong wind blows through a city filled with polluted air, the polluted air is blown away. In a similar way, when the Holy Spirit blows through us, all the things that were corrupted by Satan are blown away. The devil and his cohorts strive to fill our hearts and souls with corruption and vileness, but the wind of the Holy Spirit blows them away. Hatred, envy, jealousy, anger, lewdness, wandering, theft and so forth are blown from our hearts and minds by the Holy Spirit.

Second, when the Holy Spirit blows through us like the wind, our hearts become refreshed. Those who have been filled with the Holy Spirit no longer have worries, troubles, sadness, pain and suffering in their hearts, but instead, they have happiness and peace. Joy overflows in them. Such overflowing joy overcomes all difficult situations and helps us to bear the fruit of "love, joy, peace, patience, kindness, goodness, faithfulness, gentleness and self-control" (Gal. 5:22–23).

Third, the wind is dynamic. The Holy Spirit is an active spirit. Wind does not occur where there is no movement of the air, but rather, wind by its very nature *is* the movement of the air. Where the wind of the Holy Spirit blows, we can observe great movements and activities. When the Holy Spirit blows through us, we are motivated to spread the gospel. When the Holy Spirit blows through the church or a person, we can see movement arising from within them. A quiet church is a sign of the fact that there is no movement of the Holy Spirit.

LIKE FIRE

They saw what seemed to be tongues of fire that separated and came to rest on each of them.

—ACTS 2:3

168

There are reasons for the Holy Spirit being manifested like a fire.

First, the Holy Spirit descended like a fire so that He could burn away all sin and doubt. No matter how hard we may try, we cannot cleanse ourselves. Only when the burning fire of the Holy Spirit comes upon us can our spiritual connection with the world will be broken.

The second reason that the Holy Spirit descended like fire is to shed the bright light of heaven. Fire drives away the darkness and makes things bright. Before the light of the Holy Spirit, we lived without the knowledge of heaven in a dark and gloomy world. But with the coming of the Holy Spirit, our hearts were brightened.

The third reason that the Holy Spirit descended like fire is to make our hearts burn. For our faith to become burning hot we must be filled with the Holy Spirit. When the Holy Spirit dwells within us, we can pray fervently, worship the Lord with reverence and sincerity and become eager witnesses for Jesus Christ.

The fourth reason that the Holy Spirit descends like fire is to give us a powerful faith. When the Holy Spirit dwells within us, we are no longer powerless Christians, but we become Christians with overflowing power and ability.

WITH THE MANIFESTATION OF TONGUES

**All of them were filled with the Holy Spirit
and began to speak in other tongues as the
Spirit enabled them.**
−Acts 2:4

Speaking in tongues refers to the state of glorifying God and the spreading of God's kingdom through the power of the Holy Spirit. Sometimes we make the mistake of thinking that our speaking in tongues and our having the ability to be a dynamic witness for Christ comes from within our own being.

We must realize that these two things are only possible through the Holy Spirit. Speaking in tongues is not within our control, but it is the Holy Spirit talking through our mouths. This is the reason why people who do not have the gift of speaking well in front of others can at times become eloquent and powerful when the Holy Spirit fills them.

When I was attending theology school, there was a female student who was very shy and quiet. She could not even raise her face to look others in the eyes. But when she was filled with the Holy Spirit, a great change came over her. That shy girl joined us in our crusades around the city. When we reached a park, the shy girl began preaching the gospel in a loud voice that rang throughout the park. Many people heard her preaching and were moved by her words. She was transformed. The Holy Spirit takes control of our hearts and mouths and turns a person who cannot speak well into someone who can deliver Christ's message effectively and powerfully.

Speaking in tongues implies God's desire for us to spread the gospel in every language to all people in this world. The Holy Spirit is the Spirit of evangelism. When we are filled with the Spirit of evangelism, the Holy Spirit, the consequence is a desire to evangelize not only our neighbors, but also the world. The Holy Spirit blows through us to clear away all the things in our hearts polluted by sin and instills a burning faith within us. He then uses us as powerful witnesses to spread the gospel.

BEING FILLED WITH THE HOLY SPIRIT

Jesus Christ made a promise to the disciples before His death concerning the baptism by the Holy Spirit. After His resurrection, Jesus appeared to the disciples who were in hiding and urged them to receive the Holy Spirit. As Jesus ascended to heaven, He told His followers, "Do not leave Jerusalem, but wait for the gift my Father promised, which you have heard me speak about. For John baptized with water, but in a few days you will be baptized with the Holy Spirit" (Acts 1:4–5).

In obedience to Jesus Christ, His followers gathered together in Jerusalem to pray. They experienced the coming of the Holy Spirit on the Day of Pentecost, just as Jesus Christ had promised. Since that day, the Holy Spirit dwells among those who believe in Christ. What are the benefits of being filled with the Holy Spirit?

PEACE, EAGERNESS AND DEEP FELLOWSHIP

After Christ's ascension, His disciples prayed together for ten days. On the Day of the Pentecost, they experienced the coming of the Holy Spirit like wind and fire. Each person began speaking in tongues.

Although many people confess that they believe in Jesus Christ, they live with a sense of guilt, fear, worry, anxiety, uncertainty, despair and disbelief. However, when the Holy Spirit of Pentecost descends upon them, all these emotions disappear, and they have a wondrous peace. This is because the Holy Spirit is a wind of life and holiness that clears away sin, unrighteousness and filth.

The Holy Spirit of Pentecost is also symbolized by fire. Just as fire has a characteristic to burn away certain impurities, the fire of the Holy Spirit burns away everything that is filthy and vile. The Holy Spirit starts the flames of faith, hope and love in our hearts. Fire also symbolizes eagerness and diligence. A person filled with the Holy Spirit lives with eagerness and diligence.

When the Holy Spirit came down, Christ's followers began speaking in tongues. In comparison to regular prayers, speaking in tongues is praying on a much deeper level. Speaking in tongues makes it possible for us to pray much longer than otherwise. Being filled with the Spirit provides for us peace and eagerness, and also allows us to have a deep relationship with God.

A POWERFUL CHRISTIAN

Philip was a deacon in the church in Jerusalem and was filled with the Holy Spirit. He went down to Samaria to spread the gospel. Upon his arrival, there was a great miracle in Samaria. "With shrieks, evil spirits came out of many, and many paralytics and cripples were healed. So there was great joy in that city" (Acts 8:7–8). Wherever the gospel was preached, evil spirits were cast out of bodies, and the sick became well.

But despite all Philip's work there was not a single person who was filled with the Holy Spirit. The followers in Jerusalem heard the news that the gospel had reached Samaria. Upon hearing the news, the Jerusalem church decided to send Peter and John. Peter and John decided to pray for the coming of the Holy Spirit, and the Samaritans received and were filled with the Holy Spirit (Acts 8:14–15). Our work is not complete once we deliver the message of the gospel. We must also pray that converts are filled with the Holy Spirit.

THE KEY TO SOLVING PROBLEMS

Among the early churches the church at Antioch was the largest. It was able to grow to such greatness because there was a close and rigorous communication with the Holy Spirit. To maintain such close contact with the Holy Spirit, the members of the church at Antioch continuously fasted and prayed to God. As a result, they became powerful witnesses of the gospel.

Today, many Christians are not able to experience the power of the Holy Spirit because they do not wholly depend on God, but rather they depend on themselves. They are filled with questions such as, "What shall I eat?" "What shall I wear?" "What shall I drink?" When we wholly depend on God and through fasting and prayer seek God's kingdom and His righteousness, we shall experience the wisdom, intelligence and power of the Holy Spirit.

Wherever I spread the gospel, I always emphasize the importance of acknowledging, greeting, accepting and depending on the Holy Spirit. I do this because I need the help of the Holy Spirit to drench my mind and thoughts just as the morning dew softly and gently drenches the leaves. At times I am troubled by some problem during my ministry or crusade, but whenever I kneel in front of our Lord Jesus Christ and pray, I feel the Holy Spirit helping me to find the solution to the problems and to take away all my worries and fears. As we revere God and pray to Him while we fast, we not only experience the great power of the Holy Spirit, but we also find solutions to our problems.

To bear the beautiful fruit of our faith, we must be filled with the Holy Spirit. When we are filled with the Holy Spirit, we shall have peace and diligence like that of fire. As our fellowship with God deepens, we shall have successful lives of faith.

HOW TO BE FILLED WITH THE HOLY SPIRIT

Many people think that being born again is the same as being filled with the Holy Spirit, but there is a distinct difference between the two. Being born again refers to being born as children of God once we accept Jesus Christ as our Savior. At the time of our confession, the Holy Spirit enters into our hearts and makes it possible for us to repent and believe. "Therefore I tell you that no one who is speaking by the Spirit of God says, 'Jesus is cursed,' and no one can say, 'Jesus is Lord,' except by the Holy Spirit" (1 Cor. 12:3). For a person to be able to confess that Christ is his Savior depends not on the person's self, but upon the Holy Spirit.

"Being filled with the Spirit" refers to our whole inner

minds and hearts being filled and controlled by the Holy Spirit. Once a person has been born again, that person is not necessarily filled with the Holy Spirit. However, if we are not filled with the Holy Spirit, we do not have strength or power. Jesus said, "But you will receive power when the Holy Spirit comes on you; and you will be my witnesses in Jerusalem, and in all Judea and Samaria, and to the ends of the earth" (Acts 1:8). The power mentioned in this passage is the Greek word *dunamis. Dunamis* in English is "dynamite." When we are filled with the Holy Spirit, we receive dynamite-like power.

Christians who were filled with the Holy Spirit on the Day of Pentecost were completely transformed, and they rushed out to the streets. A cowardly person was transformed to a bold person, the powerless to the powerful. As these transformed Christians boldly proclaimed the gospel, there was a lot of commotion on the streets of Jerusalem. Their prayers were like dynamite, their preaching like powerful bombs, and the result was that three thousand people repented and accepted Christ as their Savior.

If the followers of Christ were not filled with the Holy Spirit, Christianity might not have survived. But because the Holy Spirit descended on each, the prayers and preaching of the believers became as powerful as dynamite, and the gospel was spread throughout the world. To be filled with the Holy Spirit is to receive God's power, and for those who wish to become servants of Christ, being filled with the Holy Spirit is an absolute necessity. What must we do to be filled with the Holy Spirit?

A Christian may ask, "Could a person such as I be filled with the Holy Spirit?" The Word of God answers this question.

Repent and be baptized, every one of you, in the name of Jesus Christ for the forgiveness of your sins. And you will receive the gift of the Holy Spirit. The promise is for you and your

children and for all who are far off—for all
whom the Lord our God will call.
—ACTS 2:38–39

In this passage "you" refers to the Jewish people, "your children" refers to the descendants of the Jewish people, and "all who are far off" refers to all people who are not Jewish. In other words, not just the Jewish people, but all can receive the Holy Spirit. This is not to say that all people will be filled with the Holy Spirit. The Holy Spirit descends on those who believe in Christ and those who have been called by God. As long as these two conditions are met, we can be filled with the Holy Spirit.

We must hold firmly to this promise. When we do so, faith begins to grow in us, and the Holy Spirit will do His work through us.

POSSESS A BURNING DESIRE

When we understand how beneficial being filled with the Holy Spirit is, the desire to have the Holy Spirit begins to burn in us.

Christians who live without being filled with the Holy Spirit do not have joy and peace flowing from their hearts. They find it difficult to pray, their witnessing is ineffective, and no matter how much they desire, the Word of God does not seem sweet to their ears. They even go so far as to think that believing in Christ is difficult. When we are filled with the Holy Spirit, peace overflows in our hearts. Our prayers, witnessing and words take on the power of God. We are empowered to overcome the world as well as Satan, allowing us to live in victory.

It took me two years to be filled with the Holy Spirit. When I first began praying for the Holy Spirit, I really didn't have the burning desire in my heart. So when my prayers went unanswered, I often gave up easily and said to myself, "Oh, there will be other opportunities in the future."

It was not until my second year in my theological studies that I experienced being filled with the Holy Spirit. At the time, I at least knew intellectually the benefits of being filled with the Holy Spirit. Some other students and I went up to a mountain to pray earnestly for the Holy Spirit. I started my prayer with a strong determination that I would not leave the mountain until I was filled with the Holy Spirit. To my great surprise, not more than five minutes after I began to pray, I was filled with the Holy Spirit. To be filled with the Holy Spirit, we must pray with the burning desire of the heart and a strong determination of the mind.

REPENT OF SIN

To receive the Holy Spirit, we must first repent our sins. Through many years of living in disobedience to God's will, our hearts have become hardened. We must seek God's help so that He can break our hearts and our disobedience to Him. Afterwards, we must repent of every sin we committed since our childhood and pray for cleansing through the blood of Jesus Christ.

To be filled with the Holy Spirit, we must devote all our hearts and bodies completely to this cause. "O Holy Spirit, I give myself to you. Come and occupy me completely." After we have prayed thus, we must pray, "O Lord God, thank You for granting me the Holy Spirit." Jesus Christ said, "If you then, though you are evil, know how to give good gifts to your children, how much more will your Father in heaven give the Holy Spirit to those who ask him" (Luke 11:13). Ephesians 3:20 says, "Now to him who is able to do immeasurably more than all we ask or imagine, according to his power that is at work within us." As we seek the Holy Spirit through our prayers, God blesses us and fills us with the Holy Spirit.

However, there is a unique sign that marks our being filled with the Holy Spirit. Different people have different signs when filled with the Holy Spirit. Some feel bodily trembling, and some feel a burning sensation. There are those who do not feel any such signs. However, there is one unique thing shared by all. When we are filled with the Holy Spirit, peace and joy begin to overflow from our hearts. Additionally, our prayers begin to become more and more powerful, and we begin to speak in tongues. But being filled with the Holy Spirit once does not mean that we will always be filled with the Holy Spirit.

We must always be filled with the Holy Spirit, and we must put our best efforts forward to bear the fruit of the Holy Spirit. Only then can we become servants of Christ and be used by God.

FOUR STEPS TO BEING FILLED WITH THE HOLY SPIRIT

In the Old Testament, there was a prophet named Elijah. Being filled with the Holy Spirit, Elijah was able to perform miracles in the name of God. He ascended to heaven without succumbing to death. The work Elijah did before his ascension to heaven teaches us some important lessons.

God had preplanned Elijah's ascension to heaven. For the culmination of His purpose, God led Elijah from Gilgal through Bethel and Jericho and finally to Jordan. During Elijah's journey from Gilgal to Jordan, his disciple, Elisha, did not leave his side. He stayed with him throughout the journey. Elijah asked Elisha, "Tell me, what can I do for you before I am taken from you?" To this, Elisha replied, "Let me inherit a double portion of your spirit" (2 Kings 2:9).

Elisha was filled with the Holy Spirit just as he had desired, and he became a prophet who is credited with saving Israel. By looking at Elisha as he followed Elijah, we can learn the steps to take as we live in faith filled with the Holy Spirit and experiencing the wonders of God's blessings and power.

THE FIRST STEP—"FAITH LIKE THAT AT GILGAL"

Elisha's journey following after Elijah began in Gilgal. Gilgal was to be the place where Elisha would miraculously purify a poisoned stew so that one hundred of his followers could eat (2 Kings 4:38–41). Gilgal was where one of God's miracles took place. "Faith like that at Gilgal" is having faith that allows us to experience God's miracles.

In order for us to be filled with the Holy Spirit, we must believe in God who did and can perform miracles. Some say, "The miracles in the Bible are mere myths. The Bible is nothing more than a book, a novel, written by man. We must not credit the Bible with anything more than its cultural, philosophical and ethical value." There are many pastors and spiritual leaders who plant the seeds of these dangerous thoughts in the minds of their people. This is not according to God's will. God desires that each of us have "faith like that at Gilgal."

"Faith like that at Gilgal" refers to faith that believes the Bible exactly as it is written. The miracles in the Bible happened exactly as written, and they can happen to us even today. We must have the faith that wholly believes in the miracles in the Bible as well as the promises made by God in the Bible.

When we turn our backs on a man-centered humanistic view of Christianity and our faith becomes like that at Gilgal, we have taken the first step to experiencing the filling of the Holy Spirit.

THE SECOND STEP—"FAITH LIKE THAT AT BETHEL"

As they were leaving Gilgal, Elijah said to Elisha, "Stay here; the LORD has sent me to Bethel" (2 Kings 2:2). Elisha swore that he would not leave Elijah's side. Elisha accompanied Elijah to Bethel. To receive the power of the Holy Spirit, we must not remain at Gilgal, but we must press on to Bethel.

The name *Bethel* means "God's house." When we search the Bible, we can see the deeper meaning associated with Bethel. Bethel is the place where Abraham, having left his father's house and land, entered Canaan and built an altar to God. Bethel is also the place where Jacob built an altar to God after his vision through a dream. Bethel was the place where God's chosen ones built altars to Him and made covenants with the Lord.

Our Bethel is under the cross of Calvary. We may acknowledge the great power of our God, but it does not mean that we will experience that power. We will come to experience the great power of God through the Holy Spirit when we come before the altar built upon the blood of Jesus Christ. Those who acknowledge and believe in the power and miracles of God but fail to come to church and worship Him are those who have remained behind in Gilgal and have failed to reach the next step in their faith, "faith like that at Bethel."

We must come before the cross of Jesus Christ and find reconciliation with God through the blood of Jesus Christ. Then we must go to church and build our altars to the Lord God, and we must continue building our altars in our daily lives. When our faith has reached such a status, we can be said to have reached the faith of Bethel. When we have reached the faith of Bethel, we have taken a further step toward experiencing the power of the Holy Spirit.

The third step—"Faith like that at Jericho"

Elijah said to Elisha again, "Stay here, Elisha; the LORD has sent me to Jericho" (2 Kings 2:4). He commanded Elisha to stay behind in Bethel, but Elisha refused and continued to follow Elijah. If we desire to experience and receive the power of the Holy Spirit, we must take a further step toward Jericho.

Jericho was the first city that barred the Israelites in their journey to Canaan. For the Israelites, their living in and obtaining Canaan, the land where honey and milk flowed, depended on their ability to conquer the great city of Jericho. To conquer this city, the Israelites obeyed God's command to march around the city once a day. On the seventh day, they marched around the city seven times, and on the seventh time they began shouting in loud voices. The hand of God came down from heaven and destroyed the great city of Jericho. "Faith like that at Jericho" refers to faith that helps us to be victorious against our enemies.

Those enemies that try to block our faith are temptation and hardship. If we cannot overcome these enemies, we cannot experience the great power of God. For us to be victorious over temptations and hardships, we must arm ourselves with God's Word and prayer. When we go to battle boldly, armed with God's Word and prayer, obstacles such as Jericho shall be destroyed, and we shall enter into a deeper relationship with God.

THE FOURTH STEP—"FAITH LIKE THAT AT JORDAN"

Elijah said to Elisha at Jericho, "Stay here; the LORD has sent me to Jordan" (2 Kings 2:6). Elisha pleaded earnestly to accompany Elijah to the end of his journey. Elijah was unable to refuse Elisha's pleading, and they journeyed on toward Jordan together.

Jordan is a natural river barrier that served as a border to Canaan. The Israelites, after having been brought out of Egypt, were judged by God and were denied their entrance into Canaan because of their disobedience to God. As a result, all Israelites who were brought out from Egypt died in the desert. Those whom God allowed to cross Jordan into Canaan were Joshua and Caleb, who had obeyed God.

"Faith like that at Jordan" is faith that helps us to abandon our own wills and desires and completely give ourselves to the will of God. In other words, "faith like that at Jordan" refers to our abandonment of a man-centered humanistic faith and the full acceptance of a God-centered faith.

A great reward awaited Elisha. He became a power-filled prophet. When we live with God at the center of our being and wholly obey God's words, we will be filled with the Holy Spirit and will become powerful Christians. When our faith continues to grow, we shall be filled with the Holy Spirit and become powerful Christians.

O Lord, help us to live according to Your will as we are filled with and led by the Holy Spirit. Thank You for helping us to realize that being filled with the Holy Spirit is Your will. It is our heart-filled desire to be filled with the Holy Spirit so that our faith can continue to grow in Jesus Christ. Lead us from Gilgal, through Bethel and Jericho, to Jordan, so that with the power of the Holy Spirit we can become Your power-filled servants and glorify You. In Christ's name, amen.

FIFTEEN

The Evidence of the Holy Spirit

Amid great chaos and void the Spirit of God, the Holy Spirit, moved and began the great miracle of Creation (Gen. 1). After the resurrection and ascension of Jesus Christ, the Holy Spirit came to the world on the Day of Pentecost. The Holy Spirit continues to do His great work among Christians today through the church. Exactly what work does the Holy Spirit do for us?

THE HOLY SPIRIT BRINGS FREEDOM

After Adam and Eve fell, a terrible "poverty," both spiritual and physical, came to afflict mankind. Fallen man no longer knew where he had come from, why he was living or where he was headed. In this state of despair and ignorance, he wandered from place to place. With his communication with God severed, his heart was filled with emptiness and confusion. The physical world was condemned, and instead of producing that which is beneficial to man, there grew thorns and thistles. In order for man to sustain himself from this condemned land, he had to etch a living through sweat, a tragic situation when compared to that before his Fall.

However, when we believe in Jesus Christ and the Holy Spirit dwells within us, all of this changes. God pours His blessings upon us and drives away poverty and destitution. The Holy Spirit not only enriches our personal lives, but He also enriches our families, societies and nations.

The Holy Spirit brings freedom. Satan and his cohorts try to steal, kill, destroy and make prisoners of our spirits. The Holy Spirit unties and destroys Satan's noose and gives us freedom. Where the Holy Spirit resides, there is freedom.

Many people have become Satan's prisoners. Not a single person can escape from this prison on his or her own. Satan leads his prisoners to depart from God and teaches them to live according to fleshly and carnal desires. He leads them to eternal condemnation. However, when the Holy Spirit does His work within the people, all the chains and restraints that Satan had used to bind them will be destroyed instantaneously. "Now the Lord is the Spirit, and where the Spirit of the Lord is, there is freedom" (2 Cor. 3:17). When we live our lives with the Holy Spirit within us, read God's Word every day and pray to Him, the Holy Spirit grants us freedom from Satan's power and authority.

THE HOLY SPIRIT BREATHES LIFE

Before Adam sinned against God, his body and spirit were both open to God, and he was able to commune and have fellowship with God. But after his fall from God's grace, he faced spiritual and physical death. All descendants of Adam inherited death and were born with a dead spirit.

Mankind could not see or know of the spiritual world, but only the physical, material world. Man had become a materialistic being. There have been many extremists who claim,

"There is no god." They insist there is neither God nor heaven. They believe that there is only the life on this earth and that each man should try his best to fully enjoy his life while in this world. They have absolutely no knowledge of the meaning of life.

These people can have amazing changes come over them when the Holy Spirit descends upon them. The Holy Spirit breathes life into their spirits through the gospel and opens their spiritual eyes. Those whose spiritual eyes have been opened come to realize that God is alive and that Jesus Christ is their Savior. They no longer live wandering from place to place, but they live with a desire to become witnesses for the gospel. They live with a desire for the new world, the new Jerusalem.

The Holy Spirit also frees us from our burdens. Only in God can we find true freedom. The Holy Spirit frees us from the burdens of our sins, from the sense of guilt and from our mental and emotional anguish. He cures us of all our ills, both emotional and physical, and fills us with a peace that transcends our understanding.

THE HOLY SPIRIT TRANSFORMS

The blessed year refers to the year of the Jubilee. God had commanded the Israelites to observe the year of the Jubilee—the blessed year. The year of the Jubilee came every fifty years after seven sabbatical years. When the year came, those who had sold their land or cows because of hardship could reclaim their property, and those who had been sold into slavery could find their freedom. When the trumpet of Jubilee sounded, it converted sadness to happiness, despair to hope.

Jesus Christ came into the world to announce the year of Jubilee. After Christ's death and His ascension, the Holy Spirit came to announce the beginning of the Jubilee year. The Holy Spirit continues to make the same announcement.

We have been freed from sin through the blood of Jesus Christ, and we have returned to the warm embrace of God.

When the Holy Spirit descends upon us, we come to have faith in the Lord Jesus Christ, and there is a miracle of creation and healing in us. When we continue to seek and ask the Holy Spirit for such experiences, we become victorious.

THE FRUIT OF THE HOLY SPIRIT

When we believe in Jesus Christ and accept Him, the Holy Spirit comes to reside in our hearts and makes us bear nine different fruits. Jesus Christ teaches us how to bear the fruits through the illustration of the grapevine.

Remain in me, and I will remain in you. No branch can bear fruit by itself; it must remain in the vine. Neither can you bear fruit unless you remain in me. I am the vine; you are the branches.
–JOHN 15:4–5

Also, Jesus said that God is glorified when we bear much fruit for Him. When we reside in Christ, what spiritual fruits does the Holy Spirit produce in us?

THE FRUIT OF LOVE

The love that the Holy Spirit gives is not the same as the love between man and woman, which is the Greek word *eros,* nor is it the love between friends, which in Greek is *philio.* It is not the love between parents and children, known in Greek as the word *stolkae.* Although there are some differences in degree among such "loves," these loves are conditional. However, the love that the Holy Spirit gives is the love of God, the Greek word *agape.* This is the love that sacrifices. *Agape* is unconditional love given with no thought of return.

We must pray that we can bear this fruit of *agape* love in our daily lives through the Holy Spirit.

The Fruit of Joy

The joy that the Holy Spirit gives is fundamentally different from the happiness that is achieved through attainment of wealth or fame, or through some physical satisfaction. The joy that the Holy Spirit gives us comes through grace. This fruit of joy grows in us when we revere the Word of God and Christ. The joy grows when we pray every day in faith.

The Fruit of Peace

The peace that the Holy Spirit brings is not peace that comes from living in a peaceful environment. A rich man invited many famous painters to his house. He offered to pay handsomely for the painting that best depicted peace. After making this offer, he gave ample time for each painter to start painting. All the painters painted as best as they could, and each painter displayed his painting for the rich man.

The first painter's work depicted a peaceful countryside. The rich man looked at the painting for a few minutes and passed on. The second painting was a beautiful portrayal of a family that had gathered together and were talking happily. The rich man passed on. The third painting was that of a calm pond on a clear day with a clear blue sky. The rich man passed on.

The fourth painting was that of a mighty waterfall like Niagara Falls. Next to the waterfall, there was a small branch growing out of the rocks. On that branch, there was a mother eagle sitting on her eggs in the nest in complete contentment.

The rich man stood transfixed with his eyes focused on the painting. He selected the painting of the waterfall and the eagle. When the other artists began questioning his decision, the rich man quietly said, "Look at the mother eagle's eyes as she sits on top of her eggs. She has no fear, only peace. She could be swept into the waterfall at any time. In the same way, we ourselves do not know when a disaster will strike, but if we have peace like this mother eagle, we have true peace."

The fruit of peace that the Holy Spirit grants us is not necessarily bound to a peaceful environment, but peace granted by God comes from deep within our souls regardless of our environment. Only this peace can overcome fear and dread and give us strong faith and courage.

THE FRUIT OF PATIENCE

Patience is the foundation of faith, and God tests our patience before He blesses us. Of the qualities reflecting patience, there is long-suffering. If we have received God's Word and have absolute trust in Him, regardless of what disaster or suffering we face, we will be able to endure it through His Word.

Patience is also not doubting God's love. Job faced many indescribable hardships. He endured all his hardships and overcame the disasters through incredible patience. For his long-suffering and endurance, God multiplied Job's blessings.

Faith requires patience. We cannot obtain patience with our human strength and determination. Only when we are helped by the Holy Spirit can we have real patience.

THE FRUIT OF COMPASSION

Compassion is pity and sorrow for others. Mankind was originally created with a compassionate heart, but as sin entered compassion was lost. As a result, our hearts were filled with jealousy, envy, hatred and other undesirable emotions. Disobedience and confrontation with God began to rule our hearts.

God treats us with unlimited compassion. We discover in the Bible how Jesus with compassion rather than reproach forgave a woman caught in the act of adultery (John 8:1–11). The Holy Spirit helps us to bear the fruit of compassion and makes it possible for us to understand, pity and help others.

THE FRUIT OF KINDNESS

Kindness is having a good heart and doing good deeds for others. While there are some people in this world who are born with goodness and meekness, there are those who are violent and evil. The Holy Spirit works within people of diverse character to bear the fruit of kindness. A kind husband, a kind wife, a kind son, a kind neighbor and a kind Christian not only brighten and bring warmth and happiness to their families, but they also brighten and bring warmth and happiness to their churches and their societies. The Holy Spirit bears the fruit of kindness from within us so that we can live worthy of being called God's children.

THE FRUIT OF LOYALTY

Loyalty refers to steadfastness in any situation and unwavering conviction. Today, this kind of loyalty has become more and more difficult to find. Those of us who have received the blessing of salvation must be loyal to God and Jesus Christ no matter how the world may view our faith.

The Bible says, "Do not be afraid of what you are about to suffer. I tell you, the devil will put some of you in prison to test you, and you will suffer persecution for ten days. Be faithful, even to the point of death, and I will give you the crown of life" (Rev. 2:10). God desires our loyalty, and it is our obligation. The Holy Spirit helps us to bear the fruit of loyalty so that we may be completely loyal to God.

THE FRUIT OF MEEKNESS, GENTLENESS

Gentleness refers to a warm and soft heart that is well tamed. Wild animals that are not tamed live in constant danger and fear. The gentle animal tamed by mankind lives under the protection of man and lives comfortably. Our lives are very similar. Although we may think that the fierce and aggressive people succeed, such is not true. It is rare to find such a person living a peaceful life. On the other hand, there are many gentle and meek people living peacefully. "Blessed are the meek, for they will inherit the earth" (Matt. 5:5). God takes care of the gentle and the meek. They are not only blessed while they live, but they also receive God's kingdom.

THE FRUIT OF TEMPERANCE

Temperance means to suppress our greedy nature and to be satisfied with our own limitations. Too much of even good things can be bad. The Holy Spirit helps us to bear the fruit of temperance, which teaches us to know our limits and live according to those limits.

THE HOLY SPIRIT'S POWER IN THE WORK OF THE CHURCH

During His resurrection and ascension, Jesus said to His disciples, "Do not leave Jerusalem, but wait for the gift my Father promised, which you have heard me speak about. For John baptized with water, but in a few days you will be baptized with the Holy Spirit" (Acts 1:4–5).

The disciples waited for the Holy Spirit whom Jesus had promised, and they gathered together and prayed. After ten days of praying, noise like that of a great rushing wind came from the heavens, and the Holy Spirit sat atop each person like a flame. Everyone in that room was filled with the Holy Spirit and received the gift of tongues. They spoke in different languages.

Jerusalem was overflowing with people, both Jewish and Gentiles, who had come to Jerusalem to celebrate Pentecost. Peter and the other eleven apostles, being filled with the Holy Spirit, stood among the people and began to preach the gospel in loud voices. Through his preaching, Peter reached three thousand people. They believed in Jesus Christ and were baptized. The disciples became confident and began to preach the gospel everywhere. Effective evangelism requires the Holy Spirit.

THE SPIRIT WHO WITNESSES

The first missionary was Jesus. The Bible says, "Jesus went

through all the towns and villages, teaching in their synagogues, preaching the good news of the kingdom and healing every disease and sickness" (Matt. 9:35). Jesus Christ came with the power and authority of God and taught the people about God's kingdom.

After Jesus Christ completed God's plan for mankind's redemption and ascended to heaven, the Holy Spirit came to this world to help spread the gospel. Jesus Christ had told the disciples this before His death. "But when he, the Spirit of truth, comes, he will guide you into all truth" (John 16:13).

The Holy Spirit is the central figure in the spread of the gospel. The Holy Spirit calls all of us who would work for Christ to become missionaries to go into the world and be bold witnesses. Through our witnessing, the hearts of listeners will be opened. Through belief in Jesus Christ the lost will be made righteous, and by confessing their faith with their mouths, they will receive salvation.

Spreading the gospel cannot be done through man's wisdom alone. Spreading the gospel is only possible through the work and power of the Holy Spirit. We must never forget that the master in charge of evangelism is the Holy Spirit.

CHRIST'S HEART AND EVANGELISM

Jesus cast aside the glory of heaven and came down to this wretched world in a physical body to suffer and be tempted in the same way that we are. He suffered to save lost sheep. Jesus Christ was nailed on the cross and shed His blood so that we could be saved from sin and death.

During the nineteenth century, there was a missionary from England named Hudson Taylor. He traveled to China to do missionary work. At the young age of twenty-eight, he was blessed by God and burned with God's calling to take the gospel to inner China where the gospel had not yet reached. At the time, China had closed all its doors to prevent foreign cultures from making any inroads. Within China there was much civil unrest and dispute, which made the work of the missionary difficult. No matter what the difficulties, Taylor did not give up, but rather immersed himself in methods that would enable him to turn the Chinese around and bring them to God.

He decided to become a Chinese himself. He immediately grew his hair long so that he could tie his hair in the way of the Chinese. He learned the Chinese language so that he could speak to them, and he wore the clothes of the Chinese. Having transformed himself, he went among the Chinese people to laugh and cry with them, treat their illnesses and teach the Bible. When he did so, the Chinese, one by one, began to turn to God. As a result of his efforts, a great evangelical movement began in China.

The most important quality for those who preach the gospel is having the heart and mind of Jesus Christ.

Who, being in the very nature of God,
did not consider equality with God
something to be grasped, but made himself
nothing, taking the very nature of a servant,
being made in human likeness. And being
found in appearance as a man, he humbled
himself and became obedient to death
—even death on a cross!
—PHILIPPIANS 2:6–8

When we witness for Christ, we must have Christ's humility and burning love. We must have pity for the souls that are headed toward death, and we must become seeds of hope (John 12:24).

PRAYER AND WITNESSING

The Holy Spirit is the Spirit of evangelism. As a result, the church that is filled with the Holy Spirit becomes a central figure in evangelism, and a Christian who is filled with the Holy Spirit becomes a witness.

However, the work of evangelism can only be done through prayer. We can see a clear example of this when we look at the church of Antioch in the Book of Acts. As the members of the Spirit-filled church at Antioch prayed while fasting, they received the command from the Holy Spirit, "Set apart for me Barnabas and Saul for the work to which I have called them" (Acts 13:2). In obedience to the order of the Holy Spirit, they ordained Barnabas and Saul and dispatched them as missionaries. This was the springboard to spread the gospel throughout Asia Minor.

The Holy Spirit spreads the gospel throughout the whole world by employing a church that prays. This is the very reason why the apostle Paul strongly urged the Christians of Colossi, "Pray for us, too, that God may open a door for our message, so that we may proclaim the mystery of Christ, for which I am in chains" (Col. 4:3).

We must not only pray for the missionaries who have gone out to all parts of the world to establish new churches, but we must also support them so that the mission of evangelizing the world can continue and expand. Every Christian is called to be a missionary, but there are other ways we can witness. We can witness by praying, and we can witness by giving. Prayer and giving are two essential ingredients in the work of evangelism. Missionary work is God's holy will and our responsibility. We must pray continually, and we must take on the humble likeness of Christ's heart and put all our efforts to evangelism.

O God, we pray that the power of the Holy Spirit will be manifest among us and that He will descend upon us now with all His authority and power. Help us to glorify You by continually bearing the fruit of the Holy Spirit in our lives as we are led by the Holy Spirit until the day we die. We ask that You fill us with the Holy Spirit so that we may put our best efforts toward witnessing in all the world. In Christ's name, amen.

SIXTEEN

The Life of the Holy Spirit

Many Christians do not know God's will and plans, but they live according to their own wisdom and methods. Living according to one's own wisdom will not only fail to please God or accomplish God's will, but it will also bring disappointment and failure.

This mistake is not limited to those who are "baby" Christians, but even those who have strong faith and participate in serving the church and the gospel. In Acts 16 there is a story of how the Apostle Paul faced failure due to his having followed his own will.

HOW TO LIVE ACCORDING TO GOD'S WILL

Even apostles and evangelists can fall into the trap of following their own humanistic wisdom and plan. What must we do to abandon the humanistic methods and accomplish God's will?

ABANDON OUR IMPATIENCE

Jesus promised His disciples, "And I will ask the Father, and he will give you another Counselor to be with you forever" (John 14:16). The "Counselor" in this passage refers to the "one who has been called upon for help and resides beside." The Holy Spirit came to help those who believe in Jesus Christ.

Furthermore, because the Holy Spirit is the Spirit of God, He contains within Him the will and the wisdom of God. "But God has revealed it to us by his Spirit" (1 Cor. 2:10). When we acknowledge, greet, accept and depend on the Holy Spirit, He not only helps us, but He also reveals the things that God has planned and prepared for us.

However, we at times fail to depend on this great Holy Spirit, and we impatiently head off in the direction of our own will and face failure and disappointment.

In Acts 16:6–7 the Bible says, "Paul and his companions traveled throughout the region of Phrygia and Galatia, having been kept by the Holy Spirit from preaching the word in the province of Asia. When they came to the border of Mysia, they tried to enter Bithynia, but the Spirit of Jesus would not allow them to." The apostle Paul did not heed the voice of the Holy Spirit, but headed off in a direction of his own choosing.

Even today there are some Christians who do not listen to the Holy Spirit. They bring forward their own thoughts and plans. We must abandon our hasty desire to act. We must depend and wait for the Holy Spirit.

When we live in obedience to the Holy Spirit, God takes charge of our lives. We must not hastily overtake the Holy Spirit. Rather, we must wait for the will of the Holy Spirit to be made clear.

SHATTER OUR EGO

Paul, having failed in his endeavor to get to Asia and Bithynia, went to Troas guided by the Holy Spirit. The Holy Spirit led Paul to Troas in order to shatter Paul's ego of trusting his own fervor. For those who depend on their own egos, the Holy Spirit leads them to Troas. Paul entered Troas at night. The "night" at Troas not only refers to the phase of the day, but it also signifies the hardships of a person's life. Paul experienced the complete shattering of his ego amid this dark night.

God gives purpose to those who have been broken in this way, and He uses such people for His work. God shattered Paul so that He could use Paul. In the same way, a person who desires to be used by God cannot escape such complete shattering prior to being called. When we walk through such dark nights of tribulation and despair, we must abandon all human wisdom and methods. "O Father, I repent my sin of placing my will before Yours. Forgive me of my sin. I will only follow Your will from now on." When we pray in this way, God will look upon us and open a clear and bright path for us to walk down.

HAVE A DREAM

As Paul spent the dark night in Troas and repented of his sin, Christ gave him a vision, a dream. Paul had a dream of a Macedonian calling, "Come to Macedonia and help us." After his dream-vision, Paul knew that preaching the gospel in Macedonia was the will of the Holy Spirit.

God builds and fosters the faith of Christians through dreams and visions. Dreams and visions are ingredients for changing the world and bringing about a manifestation of a new world. Many people believe that money, youth and authority are the ingredients for bringing about great changes in a person's life. This is a tragic mistake. They are nothing more than mere clouds in the sky that have no solid substance. We must grab firmly onto the dreams and visions that God gives and believe that the visions and dreams will come true.

When we pray, "O my Lord Jesus Christ, I willingly abandon all of my humanistic pride and plans. From this moment, I will live for You, I will die for You. Do as You will"; when we obey the voice of Jesus Christ with complete humility, He will grant us a "new dream."

Those who set out in life without any dreams or visions are not unlike a person planning to cook a meal without ingredients. Those who desire to go down a path with the Holy Spirit must live with dreams and thoughts of, "I have been made a new creation. I have been filled with the Holy Spirit. I have been blessed and freed from condemnation. I shall live eternally with Jesus in heaven."

When our egos and prides have been completely shattered, God grants us wondrous visions and dreams, and He creates us and our lives anew according to His will.

LIVE YOUR LIFE THROUGH THE HOLY SPIRIT

Fallen man has been destined to live with many problems that cannot be solved with his ability alone. When we look at the history of mankind, we see again and again how man tried to solve his problems on his own.

After the flowering of the Renaissance, mankind turned away from God with a proclamation that "mankind can live without God." And the Enlightened Period in the eighteenth century brought man's rationale and intellectual judgment to great heights. Man proclaimed, "God is dead." And he decided that with science, he could build a heaven on earth.

THE HOLY SPIRIT IS OUR PROBLEM-SOLVER

All of the humanism failed to turn this world into utopia, but instead took it farther away.

World Wars I and II have shown the quality of mankind turning science into a tool for developing new weapons of mass destruction rather than for the welfare of mankind. Man faces exhaustion of the world's natural resources. Environmental pollution, exploding population and other such problems have driven mankind to the brink of disaster. God says, "This is the word of the LORD to Zerubbabel: 'Not by might nor by power, but by my Spirit'" (Zech. 4:6). How does the Holy Spirit provide answers to the problems that man cannot solve himself?

THE PROBLEM OF SIN

People have thought that men sin because of ignorance and poverty and that through education and raising the standard of living sin could be eradicated. Today education is being provided to almost every person, and poverty has been greatly reduced, but there has not been a comparable reduction of sin. Man's sin grows worse.

How does the Holy Spirit solve this problem? The problem of man's sin cannot be solved by his own ability, power or wealth. Only by believing in the gospel of Jesus Christ and accepting the Holy Spirit into our hearts can this problem be solved. Christianity not only provides a means for forgiveness of our sins, but Christianity also provides the means for dealing with our sinful nature.

Jesus Christ did not die on the cross to merely forgive us of the sins, but Christ died to redeem us from our sinful nature. When we accept Jesus Christ as our Savior and seek the Holy Spirit through our prayers, the Holy Spirit comes to us and gives us freedom from the shackles of sin and the attractions of our sinful nature.

THE PROBLEM OF DEATH

None of us can escape death. Birth and death apply to every person, and this is one problem that cannot be solved by man (Heb. 9:27). However, Jesus Christ has authority over life and death. He died on the cross, was resurrected and conquered death itself.

Jesus Christ said, "I am the resurrection and the life. He

who believes in me will live, even though he dies; and who-ever lives and believes in me will never die" (John 11:25–26).

When we believe in Jesus Christ and accept Him as our Savior, the Holy Spirit comes to dwell within us, pours Christ's everlasting life into our souls and leads us so that we can live with Jesus Christ for eternity. We can boldly shout, "Where, O death, is your victory? Where, O death, is your sting?" (1 Cor. 15:55). We who believe in Jesus Christ have obtained eternal life that the Holy Spirit has underwritten, and we have been given the blessed hope of looking forward to living gloriously with Jesus Christ after our physical death.

THE PROBLEM OF HATRED

The hatred that men allow to accumulate within them is destroying the sacred relationships between parents and children, teachers and students, and among friends. If man does not find a solution to this problem of hatred, no matter how much education he has, no matter how much wealth he accumulates, all is worthless.

But Jesus Christ loves us, and He died on the cross in order to provide a solution to our problem of hatred. The Bible urges, "Above all, love each other deeply, because love covers over a multitude of sins" (1 Pet. 4:8). We must pray to Jesus Christ to fill our hearts with love. If we come before Jesus Christ and ask for the Holy Spirit's help, the Holy Spirit pours Christ's love into our hearts. Then our hearts will over-flow with Christ's love, making it easy for us to drive out hatred and love others.

THE PROBLEM OF FEAR AND ANXIETY

Fear and anxiety eat away at our well-being little by little. If we do not have peace in our hearts due to fear and anxiety, we cannot be happy no matter how much fame, glory and recognition we may receive. How can we drive out fear and anxiety and be happy?

The problem of fear and anxiety can only be solved when

we arm ourselves with peace and faith that God gives through the Holy Spirit. Romans 8:28 says, "And we know that in all things God works for the good of those who love him, who have been called according to his purpose." Therefore, we must depend on the Holy Spirit at all times so that we can drive out fear and anxiety.

THE PROBLEM OF DESPAIR FROM FAILURE

Man lives in a fast-changing society, and he is driven to compete with others for his very survival. Many have tasted bitter failure and frustration. Some have reached such frustration and despair that they can no longer function. They struggle to merely survive. The depth of their despair and frustration is so great that it is impossible for them to escape. How can a person escape from despair and frustration?

The answer is by trusting in the Holy Spirit. The Holy Spirit gives new courage and comfort to people who are suffering from frustration and despair. The Holy Spirit gives courage that emboldens a person to proclaim, "I can do everything through him who gives me strength" (Phil. 4:13).

Are you mired in failure and frustration of life? Ask for the Holy Spirit's help right now. The Holy Spirit desires to help you. When you trust the Holy Spirit and hand over all of your problems to Him, He will solve all your problems.

DON'T EXTINGUISH THE FIRE OF THE HOLY SPIRIT

All of us are influenced by the culture and trends of our society. Although some people may try to escape from the ideas and rules of their contemporaries, there is a limit as to how much they can really succeed. After much struggle, they are slowly broken and swept into the "ocean" of their environment by incessant waves of the modern world.

In our time, sin and unrighteousness have pervaded to a degree that we cannot even recognize sin, and our sense of righteousness has been blunted. For us to stand in opposition to such "waves" of the modern world and live according to God's will is challenging. Through the Holy Spirit we can meet the challenge. For Christians to live righteously they must be filled with the Holy Spirit and receive His power.

Although the Holy Spirit is eternal, He also has character. Because of His nature, the Holy Spirit is happy when we acknowledge, accept and depend on Him. When we do not acknowledge, accept and depend on Him, He is driven from our hearts. What are some of the things that can drive away the Holy Spirit?

THE LOSS OF OUR DREAMS AND VISIONS

But you will receive power when the Holy Spirit comes on you; and you will be my witnesses in Jerusalem, and in all Judea and Samaria, and to the ends of the earth.
–ACTS 1:8

The Holy Spirit is not a static being. He is hard working and moves like the wind, fire and water. The Holy Spirit gives us visions and dreams, and He commands us to follow after our dreams and visions for the purpose of spreading the gospel.

If any church or Christian lacks the vision and dream of witnessing for the gospel of Jesus Christ or does not act upon their vision, the Holy Spirit will not work through them or give them power. God brings to life the faith of those who have dreams and visions of witnessing, and God does His miracles through them. As we read the Bible and pray to God for our personal lives, our families and our children, we must also pray fervently for the spread of the gospel.

PESSIMISM—NEGATIVE EMOTIONS

There are many emotions that are considered pessimistic. Two of the most common are grumbling and resentment. Grumbling can destroy harmony in a relationship. When a

Christian continues to complain to God, the relationship between God and him is negatively affected, and this causes the Holy Spirit to depart. Resentment that always blames others drives away the Holy Spirit.

Another emotion that extinguishes the Holy Spirit is hatred. To hate a person is the same as murder. It is impossible for the Holy Spirit, the giver of life, to reside within a murderer. Anger also extinguishes the Holy Spirit. The Bible warns, "For man's anger does not bring about righteous life that God desires" (James 1:20).

We must make sure we wash away all of these negative emotions. They extinguish the Holy Spirit.

IDOLATRY

Idolatry is adultery of the spirit. As Christians, we are betrothed to Jesus Christ spiritually. We must commit all of our hearts, minds and wills to Him.

Many make the mistake of thinking that idolatry is only limited to worshiping something that can be seen with the eyes, such as some statue. However, the Bible says that greed is idolatry (Col. 3:5). In other words, if there is anything in our hearts that we deem more important or valuable than God, this is idolatry. Through the Ten Commandments, God has established that idolatry is a sin and that whosoever should commit idolatry will die.

We can see a very good example of this in Acts 5:1-11. Ananias and Sapphira were members of the church in Jerusalem. After hiding some of their wealth, they brought the rest of their property to Peter and lied to him that they had brought all of their wealth to him. They lost their lives. The reason that God judged them harshly and took their lives was because their greed led them to lie to the Holy Spirit.

Those who try to lie to the Holy Spirit will only have Him depart from them, and they will receive God's judgment. We must not only throw away all visible idols, but we must also cast aside the idols in our hearts.

OBSCENITY

God is holy and does not condone obscenity.

It is God's will that you should be sanctified: that you should avoid sexual immorality; that each of you should learn to control his own body in a way that is holy and honorable, not in passionate lust like the heathen, who do not know God.
—1 THESSALONIANS 4:3–5

The bodies of the Christians are temples of the Holy Spirit. Obscenity defiles and makes our bodies filthy. In other words, obscenity makes God's temple filthy. We must not drive away the Holy Spirit with obscenities.

SECULAR INDULGENCE

We are surrounded by secularism. If we are not careful, we may become victims of secularism and drive away the Holy Spirit. God desires each of us to be alert as we go through the world and to always seek the holiness of God.

God desires that we live filled with the Holy Spirit. God has said, "I am the LORD who brought you up out of Egypt to be your God; therefore be holy, because I am holy" (Lev. 11:45). And Hebrews 12:14 teaches us, "Make every effort to live in peace with all men and to be holy; without holiness no one will see the Lord."

When we think secular thoughts, speak with such thoughts, seek after worldly desires and indulge in the world, the Holy Spirit has no choice but to depart from us. If we desire Him to dwell within us, we must seek to be holy in our words, actions and lives.

LAZINESS CONCERNING OUR FAITH

The power and the works of God come to us through His

Word. When we ignore God's Word, we cannot experience the power of the Holy Spirit. Many Christians make the mistake of seeking to experience the Holy Spirit through some emotional enlightenment. As stated, the Holy Spirit has emotions, but being filled with the Holy Spirit is more than an emotional experience. When we read the Bible and revere its content, and when we live according to the Bible, the Holy Spirit works within us.

When we ignore the Word and prayer, the Holy Spirit departs from us. Without praying, we cannot commune with the Holy Spirit. Just as we must continue to meet and talk with those with whom we desire to maintain a close relationship, we must desire a relationship with the Holy Spirit.

When fleshly desires, carnal yearnings and pride enter our hearts, we cannot experience the work of the Holy Spirit. To experience the Holy Spirit we must have dreams and visions, seek after holiness, read the Bible and pray to the Lord.

O Lord God, we abandon all our impatience and stand before You as we repent. We wish to live with complete and undivided dependence on the Holy Spirit, and we earnestly ask for the guiding hand of the Holy Spirit. Lead us so that we can live with the power of the Holy Spirit and live victoriously day by day. In Christ's name, amen.